FINDING YOUR CHURCH

By Don H. Otto

Rardin Graphics   Charleston, Illinois   1994

Copyright 1994 Don Henry Otto
Cover by Lynn Trank

ISBN 1-886349-00-2
Library of Congress Number 202-707-5000

Note: Abingdon Press has kindly granted permission for the use of a quotation from **The Interpreter's Bible** (Volume VII) in Chapter One of Part One of this book and to summarize the characteristics of a Christian in Chapter Three of Part Two from the same source.

A PREFATORY NOTE

The author of this book thanks the churches visited and the pastors interviewed, as listed in Appendix A. He also thanks the pastors and others who have read all or part of the present version or of an earlier version. He has listened carefully to their suggestions and has tried to make prudent changes wherever possible. Nevertheless, the opinions expressed in this book are those of the author and should not be attributed to any denomination or to any member thereof. Those who have read the book and have made suggestions are members of the following denominations: Alliance, American Baptist, Community, Disciples of Christ, Presbyterian, Roman Catholic, Southern Baptist, United Church of Christ and United Methodist. Thanks to all.

The author's late wife, Jessie Brydon Otto, stimulated his renewed interest in the subject in the long discussions they had in her final days. His present wife, Glorine Harris Otto, demonstrated great patience and understanding in their one hundred visits to churches of various types as well as in the many days in which he prepared the manuscript. He owes much to both of them.

The book is dedicated to the memory of three pastors, men who in their lives and work proved that a serious inquirer can find Christian meaning for life in any of the three main branches of Christianity in America. Those pastors, now deceased, are:

Rev. L. C. Mauck, Independent Christian Pastor,

Rev. W. Russell Shaw, Presbyterian Pastor,

Rev. Robert Voigt, Roman Catholic Pastor.

Don H. Otto
Charleston, Illinois,
July 1994

TABLE OF CONTENTS

Chapter Introduction	Chapter Title	Page

Part One: A View of the Scriptures

Chapter 1	Three Ways to Approach the Scriptures	1
Chapter 2	The Search for Happiness	13
Chapter 3	Laws for Living	17
Chapter 4	The Law in Essence	23
Chapter 5	Comfort and Strength	27
Chapter 6	Human Disobedience	29
Chapter 7	The Temptations of Christ	33
Chapter 8	Christ's Sermon on the Mount	36
Chapter 9	Following Christ	43
Chapter 10	God's Mercy and Human Mercy	47
Chapter 11	The Incarnation	49
Chapter 12	Mainly About Paul	53
Chapter 13	The Flesh and the Spirit	57
Chapter 14	Christian Love	61
Chapter 15	How Christians Should Live	65

Part Two: A Guide to Visiting Churches

Chapter 1	Why People Go to Church	69
Chapter 2	Three Ways to Christian Living	75
Chapter 3	Choosing a Pastor	89
Chapter 4	How Big a Church Should Be	95
Chapter 5	The Best Church Structure for You	99
Chapter 6	Checklist for Visiting Churches	107
Chapter 7	Christianity Works!	115
Chapter 8	A Short Reading List	123
Appendix A	Churches We Visited	127
Appendix B	Some Dangers of Theology	133

INTRODUCTION

I have written this book to help serious inquirers find the kind of Christian church that can meet their needs. Anyone who is serious about finding Christian meaning for life will be willing to spend the time necessary to complete this book and whatever else is necessary in the search for meaning. In my own study and research, I have tried to discover those things that will help the reader make sense out of what otherwise might be confusing and thereby arrive more quickly at the answers, the right answers for the individual reader.

My Qualifications

My best qualification for writing such a book is that I am relatively unbiased. I believe that any of three basic approaches to Christianity can open doors to a life of meaning. I have known and worked with living saints in Catholicism, in mainline Protestantism, and in conservative Protestantism. Growing up in a conservative church, doing undergraduate work at the Catholic college in my home town, and spending more than forty years in active service in mainline Protestant churches, I have become aware of the values as well as of the hazards of all three branches of Christianity. I hope to point those out in the pages that follow.

I have served as pastor of six small Protestant churches: Disciples of Christ, Methodist, and Presbyterian. But most of my church service has been as a layman: elder, deacon, church school teacher, church school superintendent, and chairperson or member of committees with such names as Personnel, Christian Education, Stewardship and Finance, Worship, Missions, Visitation, Evangelism, Publicity, and Buildings and Grounds. There have been other church jobs, but this list is enough to suggest the thousands of hours of meetings and of more useful kinds of service. I have learned something from these experiences.

Rare for one who has spent most of adult life as a member of the laity, I have had enough undergraduate courses to represent a minor and enough seminary courses to qualify me for a license to preach (along with a course of supervised reading in theology, church history, Christology, scripture study, and church administration.) I am certified as a full-time counselor for secondary school teaching and have done the necessary study to teach at the university level a course entitled 'The Bible as Literature.' More important, I think, I have been reading books on religion for fifty years. These have included such popular works as those by C. S. Lewis, Paul Tournier, Keith Miller, and Elton Trueblood, but also major works by Paul Tillicht, Karl Barth, Emil Brunner, and the contributors to **The Interpreter's Bible.** -- This reading list is not meant to be comprehensive, but representative of the serious reading I have done.

As an English teacher, I have had occasion to live in eight communities in six states. In those various moves, I have been a member of congregations as small as seventy members and as large as thirteen hundred. Though most of the churches I have belonged to for the past forty years have been Presbyterian, I have also been a member of Baptist, Christian, and Methodist churches, each for a year or more. Because both senior pastors and assistant pastors change from time to time, I have, as a layman, observed twenty-three members of the clergy (two senior pastors and four assistants in one congregation alone). These are in addition to clerics I have encountered in ministerial associations and in seminary classes.

Nevertheless, when I decided to write this book, I felt the need for a different kind of research, not just books or courses or even the normal experiences of the church member or pastor. I decided to visit many churches of various denominations, take notes on the visits, then follow up those visits by interviewing approximately one fifth of the pastors of those churches, choosing from among the many excellent pastors I observed persons who were representative of the principle denominations one finds in the United States. On the basis of these visits and interviews, I was able to support, in some cases, or correct, in others, conclusions I had reached through study and unorganized personal observation. The list of specific churches visited and the pastors interviewed appears in Appendix A of this book. My totals come to one hundred churches and twenty pastors; my method of grouping the churches gives me a total of thirty-three denominations. I should add that Mrs. Otto willingly accompanied me on most of these visits, but that any opinions expressed in this book are my own.

Having reviewed my qualifications for writing this book, I believe that on balance, my background is as good as that of anyone else who might write on the subject.

How to Use This Book

This book is in two parts. It may be read from beginning to end, but the reader may also pick and choose.

Part One is a brief introduction to carefully selected portions of both the Old and New Testaments. You may wish to pass this by if you feel that you already have a general grasp of the meaning of the scriptures. On the other hand, it will not take you long to read these pages and the related chapters in the Bible. If you do, you will obtain a perspective on the scriptures that should be helpful to you as you read Part Two.

Because the three main branches of Christianity in America view the scriptures somewhat differently, I have tried to explain their differences in the first chapter of Part One. The chapters that follow offer you guidance in reading **key portions** of the Bible, key portions as I see them, of course. But you do need a place to start, and I have tried to be as uncontroversial in my selection of these chapters as I can be. After you decide on a specific church in which to inquire further, you will naturally wish to consult the pastor or priest of that church for any further guidance.

In Part Two, I attempt to describe some of the values and some of the hazards of different kinds of churches, using denomination, pastor, size, and structure as matters needing some explanation. Before I begin this description, however, I spend some time in explaining the different kinds of motives that bring people to church. Only if you understand that not all churchgoers are serious inquirers, though they often have worthy reasons for going to church, can you acquire the tolerance you will need to find the right church for you. — And everyone needs a church.

At the end of Part Two, I have presented a checklist to help you in your search. The individual items on the list are explained in the preceding chapters. Finally, I have presented a short reading list, one that includes standard references for the study of the three main branches of American Christianity.

I believe that God may very well intend that churches have diversity in order to be accessible to people with diverse needs. For these reasons I have written this book.

Part One
A View of the Scriptures

CHAPTER ONE
THREE WAYS TO APPROACH THE SCRIPTURES
The Conservative Way

Sunday schools originally helped their students learn to read. It was felt that if the individual could read, then he or she could discover the central meaning of the Bible. Not only the Sunday school teachers, but many of the preachers as well, had little religious preparation except for knowing how to read. Many preachers, Sunday school teachers, and Sunday school students and graduates gave a high proportion of their limited leisure hours to reading the Bible. Many knew much of the Bible by heart; certainly the Ten Commandments, many of the Psalms and Proverbs, and long passages from the New Testament. In the early nineteenth century, it was possible for a preacher to present a rather long sermon and afterward defend its main points in discussions with members of the flock. Not everyone was an authority on the Bible, but there were enough who could consider themselves to be so that a preacher needed to be on his toes when working out the fine points of a religious discourse.

On the American frontier, there were many folks who studied the Bible carefully. It was sometimes the only book in the household, and there were few leisure demands on one's time after the long day's work was done.

With few preachers prepared in colleges, many frontier churches found it expedient to call to their pulpits ministers whose chief training for the ministry included deep commitment, but not much else except regular study of the Bible. Sometimes even these poorly prepared preachers were shared by a number of frontier churches. The Methodist circuit rider of the frontier was a well known figure. The Campbellites (now bearing such names as the Church of Christ, the Christian Church, and the Christian Church - Disciples of Christ) were very active on the American frontier, and they, too, often used the circuit rider method of sharing one preacher among two or more churches. -- Now this shortage of fully educated ministers, along with the regular Bible study of church members in frontier days, created certain traditions of lay government in American churches that are still with us today. (What has often changed in the last century is that the professional ministers have generally become better prepared and the lay members of the churches often have not studied religion to any depth. Knowing this will help you understand certain eccentricities in modern churches.)

The modern conservative churches typically have the same attitude toward the Bible that frontier churches a century ago had. They revere it. Sometimes they feel that every word of the Bible, from cover to cover, has been directly inspired by God, the Bible writers acting as secretaries taking dictation. Some conservative Christians do not go that far, but they are very reluctant to yield ground in their reverential treatment of the scriptures, for they feel that the subjective rejection of certain apparently inconsistent passages may be the first steps toward anarchy. As we shall see later, there is something in what they say. Some conservative Christians are not complete literalists. For example, they may interpret the **Song of Solomon** allegorically rather than literally, a traditional orthodox interpretation; and some feel that the word 'day' in the Genesis account of creation is meant to be something like 'step' or like an archeological age. Overall, however conservative Christians treat the Bible with great reverence, not as, say, literary scholars might treat old literary manuscripts. That reverential treatment of the Bible is the principle that distinguishes all conservative Christians from scholars in mainline denominations.

Some conservative Christians, but not all, are members of what we call creedal churches. That is, they retain from ancient times the use of the Apostles' Creed or the Nicean Creed or one of the other creeds or confessions of faith. Such a creed applies the collective wisdom of ancient church fathers to the interpretation of the Bible; each creed has its support in the Bible, of course, but each part of each creed is the result of long debate among church leaders and scholars of old. Wherever the Bible must be interpreted in more than one way, the creed steers the interpreter away from danger and into traditional meanings. One finds creeds used, for example, in the Free Methodist churches, which are conservative, as well as in the United Methodist churches, which are mainline churches. Lutherans and Presbyterians are among the groups of Christians that have both conservative and more liberal denominations within their broad fold; both liberals and conservatives use one or more creeds in their services.

On the other hand, in what are called the Christian churches (independent conservative churches originating in the American frontier movement led by Alexander Campbell and Barton Stone), no creed exists. In these, and in many other conservative churches, the following statement is still the aim: 'Where the scriptures speak, we speak; where the scriptures are silent, we are silent.' Generally speaking, the Southern Baptist denomination, the largest Protestant denomination in America, takes the same approach as the conservative Christian churches do. Many Southern Baptist churches have local covenants, agreed upon by the members of the church, but they have no creeds as such.

Oops!

I had a chance to read the galley proofs of the entire book, but did not.

On page 8, change Vex to Vox.

On page 36, it should read the first 12 verses of Matthew 5, not the first 12 chapters of Matthew.

On page 48, delete starting with "State University" (Line 6) and through " Martha was important."

On page 98, delete last paragraph.

On page 100, delete fourth paragraph.

There are other typos in the book, but none should interrupt the sense of it.

As a Christian and a professor, I know that my worst sin is probably PRIDE. This should teach me a needed lesson in humility. — I blame my weak eyes, of course.

— Don Otto

With over two hundred fifty different denominations of Christians in the United States, it is obvious that there are slight differences agreed upon by the church members or by their representatives or leaders. Here, however, we are concerned only with the approach of conservative Christians to the use of the Bible. For the considerable majority of conservative Christians, the Bible is to be treated reverently; it is the principal source of knowledge about Christian meaning for life, and each Christian is free to interpret the Bible as he or she sees fit to do so. The pastor is especially skilled in the use of the Bible as a guide to meaning for life and as a source of revealed truth for Christian preaching, but any member of a church, certainly any church officer, may challenge the preacher on the accuracy of the preacher's interpretation. — The system has worked in the past, and it can continue to work so long as Christians are serious about their study of the Bible, for it is the final authority on what Christianity is and what Christians and their churches should be.

I would be the first to point out that there are problems in literal interpretation of the Bible. (As an English teacher, I have studied poetry a good deal.) And I am aware of solutions to problems of inconsistency that make sense to me and to some other mainline Protestants. But viewing the Bible as a whole, I am personally convinced that the central Christian message is available to conservative Christians who use the Bible to search out meaning for their lives. The names of the saints I have personally known and observed who have derived their knowledge of Christianity in the way described above would fill several pages. This method can work.

The Mainline Approach to the Bible

Because there are so many denominations of Christians, I must oversimplify. That should be obvious. Yet I believe that what I have said already and what I will say in the rest of this chapter is generally true and should explain some of the puzzling phenomena that the Christian churches must exhibit to an outsider looking in.

Mainline Protestant scholars differ from conservative Christian leaders in three ways. They generally regard what I shall call 'hard science' as unquestionably true. They generally regard what I shall call 'soft science' as probably true. Because of their high regard for what they call science, they tend to treat the Bible with less reverence than conservative Christians do.

By hard science, I mean such systems as geology, astronomy, mathematics, physics, chemistry, and biology. — I know that those who work within these sciences do not have all the answers and that they have corrected some preliminary conclusions within the past half century. Yet I call these hard sciences because they seem to involve less subjective interpretation than do what I call the soft sciences.

For me, the social sciences, literary criticism, psychology, and philosophy are soft sciences. No doubt I have failed to name a few that belong here, but I believe I have cited enough to suggest what I mean by the term.

In the nineteenth century and before, hard scientists announced conclusions that indicated that the world must not be a mere six thousand years old, but millions and millions of years old, contradicting the ideas of those who took the opening of **Genesis** as a literal, scientific description of the creation of the world. During the nineteenth century, as all of us know, Darwin and others announced that human beings probably evolved from lower animals, again seeming to contradict **Genesis** as a scientific (rather than a poetic) explanation of the creation. — After some deliberation, such mainline denominations as the present-day United Methodists, United Church of Christ churches, Presbyterians (major body), Episcopalians, Evangelical Lutherans, Disciples of Christ, and American Baptists accepted the idea that **Genesis** was not intended to give a literal account of creation, but a poetic one (some prefer words like **metaphor** and **allegory** to **poetry,** in this case, but I use **poetry** and **poetic**.) As the conservative Christians would aver, once you begin saying that a particular passage is meant poetically, not literally, then where do you stop? That is a good question: Where do you stop? In seminary class, I have sometimes taken as literal what the professor has insisted was hyperbolic (poetic), and sometimes I have interpreted poetically what someone equally expert has claimed to be literal. The possibility of labeling a particular passage as poetic has saved me much grief, but I know that sometimes I have not been right. I do not say this because other mainline experts are clearly right, but because I know there are some things I do not understand. I do what I can, find answers that seem to me to be consistent with other answers, then trust in God. It is most important, I feel, to get what we call the overall picture, to approach God's meaning for ourselves as closely as possible, not to be continually concerned about details to the point that we miss the main meaning.

I recognize, then, that either the conservative or the mainline Christian approach is bound to be flawed. No one of us has the mind of God; we must work within our imperfections. But I believe that both conservative Christians and mainline Christians have the potential to approach God's truth for themselves if they seek it seriously.

Reliance on the soft sciences, however, places mainliners in a more ambiguous plight, for scriptural conclusions are often about the same kinds of things that the conclusions of the soft sciences are, and when the two sets of conclusions seem to contradict each other, Christians must decide which set of conclusions is true, deciding on the basis of what they reverence most, the Bible or the science.

It need not affect our religious lives very much if we believe that life on earth is millions of years old rather than, say, six thousand years old. It does affect our religious lives a great deal, however, if we believe that human beings are incapable of voluntary unselfish actions -- as contrasted to a human nature that can be converted to unselfish patterns of life.

Now some of the social sciences assume that normal human actions are for selfish purposes: that we act from the will to pleasure, the will to power, the will to acquire property, that only restrictive laws coupled with the will to society can keep our selfish impulses from destroying the rights of others. Some psychologists, economists, and political scientists, for examples, have contributed to such descriptions of humanity. Is a human being simply an animal whose behavior must be controlled from without?

If we consider the direction of these soft sciences, we can understand why denominational governing assemblies pass resolution after resolution and center many of their efforts on obtaining political action. Relying on the vote of a majority, on the recommendation of one or more committees, they may hope to reform the world, usually according to the latest conclusions of the leaders in the soft sciences.

The alternative is the individual's interpretation of the scriptures for his or her own complex life situations. -- But this alternative would place much trust in the possibility that the individual is governed by a soul for something of the sort, and that religion is an affair between God and the individual. Is God's voice to be heard in the scriptures? Or is God's voice to be heard in the vote of the majority of delegates attending a denominational conference?

Now all of this is too general, too abstract, to be clear to the reader. Let me turn to a soft science I know something about having taught English for thirty-eight years; I refer to the soft science of literary scholarship.

Mainline seminary scholars attempt to apply the methods of history and criticism to the scriptures, treating the books of the Bible as they would treat say, the works of Homer or Chaucer or Shakespeare. They attempt to ascertain the dates of composition of different books and the authorship of those books, just for starters. That seems reasonable.

But our methods have been uncertain and inconclusive in many instances. Let me cite some examples:

Presumably Homer lived fewer than three thousand years ago, since the time of David, long after that of Moses and his predecessors. Yet when I looked up facts about Homer some twenty years ago to help me teach a survey of world literature, I discovered that we knew no more about the poet than we did when I was in college, forty-five years ago. Then we used to laugh at the old academic joke, 'We don't know whether Homer ever lived or not; we just know he was blind.' Twenty years ago we had apparently moved forward in our knowledge of Homer's great works, **The Iliad** and **The Odyssey**. Though still uncertain, and though they did not know the identity of the authors of these two great epics, scholars now seemed to feel that they could not have been written by the same person, that they must have been written a hundred years apart. -- I have not looked into the more recent scholarship in the matter. After all, I was trying to help students to see what was in the epics, not precisely when they were written or who had written them.

When I was in undergraduate college classes in English in the late forties, we were advised that the birth year of Geoffrey Chaucer was 1340. When I looked at a standard text in the 1970's, the birth year was 1343. — For one of the three or four most important writers in the English language, and one who died less than six hundred years ago, such vagueness about birth dates seems to me to be astounding! After all, Paul, author of almost a fourth of the New Testament, lived and wrote more than three times as long ago as Chaucer.

Just in passing, **Beowulf**'s author and date of composition are unknown to us, though it was apparently put in its present form less than thirteen hundred years ago, probably seven hundred or more years after Paul's dates.

Most of us accept Shakespeare as the greatest writer in English. If royalties were paid today on the stage and screen productions of his plays, he would be a wealthy man indeed -- not including the accumulated wealth of four centuries of production. Yet serious individuals still occasionally argue that the man Shakespeare did not write the plays attributed to him (most of us accept him as the author, however.) There is a gap of several years in his early adult life, years about which we know nothing. We cannot date the first production year of his greatest play, **Hamlet**; we are not sure whether the author intended Hamlet to be thirty years old (as in the First Folio edition, for example) or much closer to adolescence (as in the first published quarto edition.) There is even debate among competent literary critics, scholars who have spent their lives in studying Shakespeare, about whether Ophelia is simply an innocent pawn, weak, but good, or a crafty, bawdy young woman. — All of this uncertainty about the greatest play of a great author who lived and wrote in our language four hundred years ago. Yet scholars make firm, self-assured statements about Paul and the gospel writers and others who wrote nineteen hundred years ago and more.

I must say that historical critical analysis of literature is not an exact science. When we in English pick and choose the interpretations and criticisms we feel are most reasonable, we should do so with an awareness of the possibility of reaching the wrong conclusions in our own studies. Yet let me mention a single instance of reliance on scholarship in the Buttrick interpretation of **Matthew** in the **Interpreter's Bible:** In his exposition of verses 3-5 of Chapter 24 (**Interpreter's Bible**, VII, p. 543), the Rev. Dr. George Buttrick, undoubtedly a good man, a good Christian, and a sensitive expositor,

says:

> *The introduction to chapters 24-25 should be read with utmost care (see above). There are at least three strands in the weaving: first, a Christian 'Little Apocalypse' written in the middle of the first century, and used both by Mark (13: 4 ff.) and by Paul (I Thess. 4:15; II Thess. 2:1-10); second Matthew's additions to and changes in that text; and, third, elements drawn directly from Christ's own words.*

If one reads the introduction to **Matthew** and the exegesis, both by Sherman Johnson, in the same book, one can see the kind of skillful, probing, inquiring scholarship that has gone into the study of **Matthew** and that has influenced Buttrick's opinions. So what is the problem? Simply that it is all based on conjecture; logical, carefully studied and reasoned conjecture, it is true, but conjecture, nevertheless. Much as we would like to, we cannot penetrate that first century, when **Matthew** was written. As Johnson says in his introduction, the first complete extant texts of the book were done in the third century. We cannot really know that Matthew rearranged and invented some of Christ's words as Buttrick and Johnson claim. Scholars conclude that Matthew and Luke used **Mark** and a source that has never been discovered, but to which scholars give the name 'the Q source'' -- Admittedly, inventing a never discovered source and calling it **Q** is one way scholars can take out of a difficulty. But in so doing, they show a heavy reliance on what I call a soft science, a systematic study no more scientific (that is, provable) than my own science of the study of literature. (I refuse to honor my own studies with the word **science**; I know other, far more competent literary scholars than I am who do the same.) Whether Christ actually said the words of the four New Testament accounts of His teaching and preaching or not is obviously important to students of religion. Yet Buttrick and Johnson seem to accept the work of scholars, even when such work tends to reject the honesty and authenticity of received texts. — In my opinion, mainline scholars and their seminary students have about as many problems to encounter in their interpretation of the Bible as conservative scholars and their seminary students have. -- I do not claim that the conservatives are right, only that they have about as much chance of being right as mainliners have.

I first realized how unstable some of the conclusions of mainline scholars can be when, in a 1950 seminary class, I encountered the reasons for Morton Scott Enslin's strong suggestions that **Ephesians** was not written by Paul, but by a later disciple of Paul's. (Enslin, **Christian Beginnings**, Harper & Bros., pp. 293-298.) A major problem with attributing the letter to Paul, as early church leaders had done, was the apparent difference in vocabulary and style between Paul's first letters and this one. As I read Enslin on the topic, I thought of the M.A. thesis in English I had completed two years before. It had been a study of the shifts in style in the writing of Laurence Sterne between 1760, when the first volumes of **Tristram Shandy** were published, and 1768, when Sterne died. Now, I do not make large claims for the findings of an M.A. thesis, though I must insist that Drs. Bjornstad and Dunn, in English, and Professor Vex the 'outside reader,' chairman of the German department at Drake, were all genuine scholars, able to find any flaws that might exist in a graduate thesis. In my thesis, I had discovered a very great shift in all of the writing of Sterne in those eight years, a shift that affected not only his novels, but his published sermons as well. During the period, Sterne had ceased to be merely a Yorkshire minister in the Anglican Church, unknown outside his county. He had become a social lion in London and a favorite of some of the leading figures in north England. If this exposure to polite society and to other parts of the world (he traveled on the Continent during this period) had been an influence on his writing habits and style, why could not Paul have been similarly influenced in style and vocabulary by his travels, his contacts with different kinds of people, and, of course, his Christian experiences? I wondered. Until that time, I had, like other members of my seminary class, been somewhat startled by the conclusions of such scholars as Dr. Enslin, of Harvard. But now, after my own first attempt at literary scholarship, I developed my first real doubts about the authority of scholars in literary studies. Since that time, I have continued to ask myself questions about the sure and certain conclusions of scholars in my own soft science. I view the conclusions of mainline preachers as approximately as inaccurate as those of the conservative preachers the mainliners sometimes sneer at. I am sorry about the sneers, and also about the entrenched hostility toward mainline scholars of some of the conservative preachers, for in their sermons the preachers of the two camps of Protestantism often say much the same thing. I believe that by either method, a serious inquirer can find Christian meaning for life. In either case, however, there are a few intellectual hurdles to deal with.

The Roman Catholic Way

Mainline Protestant scholars have few or no restrictions on their investigations. Neither have mainliners who are not scholars, if they can figure out what they are doing without three years of seminary. Conservative scholars and laypersons have certain constraints in interpretation placed on them by what their denominations say about the use of scripture. Conceivably, a mainliner may study Freudian or Jungian psychology and Dewey's theories of education and the latest fashion in sociological thought and use any or all of these in 'correcting' the apparent meaning of any portion of scripture. The Roman Catholics have somewhat different ways of approaching the Bible.

For one thing, Roman Catholics have traditionally used what Protestants call The Apocrypha in about the same way that they have used the books which Protestants include in their Bibles. Some Roman Catholic translations have differed somewhat from standard Protestant translations, too, though some Protestants and the Roman Catholics have reached agreement on some common translations. In any case, modern Catholic Bibles, except for the Apocrypha, differ only slightly from modern Protestant translations.

Without making an exhaustive survey of all points of view, I can say that, at least in many instances, probably most, Roman Catholic scholars and mainline Protestant scholars have pretty well accepted the conclusions of one another. Conservative Protestants, of course, differ.

Nowadays, a member of the Roman Catholic laity is free to read the Bible, to join ecumenical Bible study groups, and to participate in the worship services of Protestant churches.

But there remains one major difference between laypersons in Roman Catholic and Protestant groups in their study of the Bible. The official doctrines of the Roman Catholic Church are determined by the hierarchy of Pope, bishops, and priests. Laypersons are not permitted to 'make up their own religion' as they go along, relying on the careful study of the Bible. Not if they wish to remain as communicants in good standing in the Roman Catholic Church. Studying the Bible is encouraged; reaching independent and unusual conclusions is not. Although most doctrines of the Roman Catholic Church have their scriptural 'proof texts,' as Hans Kung calls them, those doctrines are determined by the expert interpretations of the Pope and the other bishops. They may be guided somewhat by lay theologians, as Hans Kung was and may still be considered, and, of course, by members of the priesthood, but the Pope and his councils of bishops have the final say. -- In one sense, this is a comforting thing for laypersons: Faced with the many complexities of interpreting scriptures, the Roman Catholic layperson can simply trust the expert wisdom of sincere, dedicated members of the hierarchy to find the best possible solution to a dilemma of interpretation. The Roman Catholic way, then, is also a sensible way for the serious inquirer to use in finding Christian meaning for life. I say this because, though I personally prefer the Protestant way, particularly the freedom of the mainline Protestant way, I recognize that one can spend an entire life in analyzing the conclusions of scholars, weighing which ones seem to make most sense, and choosing a path of one's own to Christian meaning for one's life. Perhaps I am wrong in taking on such a task, for it is so easy to make a mistake, one that an expert might not make. The Roman Catholic layperson may have the right way to approach scripture, always with a ready restraint in church doctrines to keep one from making egregious blunders.

As a matter of fact, I know some good, well intentioned Christian ministers in mainline Protestant churches who believe that Bible interpretation is so great a challenge that laypersons should really leave details of interpretation to professional ministers who have spent three or more years in seminary in addition to having completed four years of undergraduate college. And, knowing how few adult mainline church members spend much time in studying their religion, I understand this point of view. It is easier by far to become a priest and accept full responsibility for the religious thought of the laity than to expect the average church member to study religion seriously. The temptation is there.

There are problems with the Roman Catholic way to the scriptures, however. Catholics have never insisted that the Bible was the only source of guidance for Christians. They have typically included what they call tradition, what they call reason, and what they call Christian experience, either stating as much or assuming it.

Now **tradition** includes a proper reverence for the writings of the Church Fathers (early Middle Ages) and for all Catholic theologians since that time. Early theologians developed the most famous creeds (Apostles' Creed and Nicean Creed) that not only Catholics, but many Protestants accept as guides to religious interpretation and understanding. St. Augustine (about 400 A.D.) is sometimes said to have invented the Catholic Church; certainly his doctrines, as altered, are part of what the Catholics call tradition. But we should point out that his allegorical interpretation of the parables of Jesus is no longer considered a valid method by such modern authorities as Robert Stein (See **An Introduction to the Parables of Jesus**, Stein, Westminster Press, 1981, particularly page 46.) We could continue in analyzing some of the problems of that great and good Christian whom we call St. Augustine, but this one is enough to make the simple point that should be made: Tradition can both help and hinder in interpretation. The same can be said about the compromises necessary in parliamentary processes required in applying collective **reason** to religious matters. (Hans Kung describes such compromises in his **Theology for the Third Millennium** but anyone who has ever participated in political negotiations, either in church or in the community, does not need Kung to explain compromise.) An individual interpreter does not have to compromise, but may follow truth wherever it may lead; this problem is a hazard for any serious inquirer, but it is also a benefit.

Perhaps as a signal to Catholics on the possibility of merger, some Protestant denominations have stressed their reliance, too, on tradition and on reason in interpreting scripture. Yet the possibility of free individual interpretation of the Bible still exists in Protestantism; in fact, that is a traditional and reasonable principle in the history of Protestantism.

I have only suggested some of the problems in each of the three cases, for my purpose is not to destroy any of these major systems, simply to point out that each has its problems that the inquirer should beware of. But it is my personal conviction that anyone who is serious and who is willing to work hard at the task will be able to find Christian meaning for his or her life in any of these three paths.

In the remainder of the chapters in Part One, I shall present what I consider to be key portions of the Bible, enough for the inquirer to obtain some idea of what being a Christian can mean. It should be enough to help the reader to judge the messages heard in the Christian churches he or she will visit. It should be obvious, however, that almost any other serious Christian might make other selections of scripture as being representative. I do not think that those other portions would present a message much different from this one, however.

CHAPTER TWO

The Search for Happiness

Ecclesiastes 1-3

In Appendix B, I have attempted to point out some of the dangers of official interpretations of God's mind, a self-styled science called 'theology.' Yet each of us does try to find what God intends for us to do, often through the study of the scriptures, I grew up in the Campbellite tradition, and in that tradition, there was an historic distrust of all creeds, official doctrines, and catechisms. Hence, my wariness of official church resolutions and denominational doctrines, as well as my reverence for the scriptures as a main source of God's instructions to human beings.

I do not say any of this apologetically, for each of us is conditioned by early experiences. My own belief is that no human mind and no collection of human minds is sufficiently perfect to be able fully to comprehend the mind of God. Hence, I know that I am wrong in some respects, perhaps in many. I cannot give you those passages to study that will be sure to tell you in a few hours of study precisely what God wants us to do and be. I can only offer a few passages that have come to have great significance for me. Neither those passages nor my comments about them, however, should be taken to represent everything that Christianity means. — For example, in my own life, Christianity has meant quite different things to me at the ages of twenty-eight, forty-two, and seventy; perhaps there will be a still different meaning for me sometime before I die.

What follows in Part One, then, is made up of personal selections of Bible passages, together with some personal guides to interpretation of those passages; those guides are, I should be saying with some regret, my own imperfect attempts to interpret the mind of God (hence, theology!) They are meant to set you on your own search for Christian meaning for your life. I hope they do.

Ecclesiastes was written centuries before the time of Christ. It is a part of what the Jewish authorities called the 'writings,' books in what we call the Old Testament that were not given the high status in the Jewish churches of the law and the prophets, but which were considered to be of great religious significance and worthy of inclusion in the scriptures.

13

Whoever the author of **Ecclesiastes** is — ask your chosen minister or priest book is written by a keen observer of human life, particularly of the various standard paths to happiness and of those who attempt each path. Such a perceptive observer would naturally attract the admiration of gifted writers; hence, it is not surprising that some of the best known authors of the twentieth century have taken titles from **Ecclesiastes** (Hemingway's **The Sun Also Rises** and Proust's **Remembrance of Things Past**, for example.) I list the first three chapters because I am trying to keep the total of scriptural passages short, and because the ideas I wish to discuss are all in those chapters. The entire book is worth careful study.

When we make what we call 'a career decision,' we usually decide what we will give our hearts to. The speaker in **Ecclesiastes** has either observed others who have given their hearts to certain goals in life -- usually associated with careers -- or has himself done so. Some of these goals are the following: wisdom and knowledge (1:17), Pleasure (2:1), wine (2:3), great possessions (2:4-7), power and position (2:8-10), and even what we may call today self development (2:11 and elsewhere.) -- Do these life goals sound familiar? They should, for pleasure, power, status, wealth, self development, and knowledge are all advertised to the young as ways to happiness today.

The writer of **Ecclesiastes** says, after much observation, that each of these paths leads not to happiness, but to 'vanity and vexation of spirit.' (2:17.) The speaker says that after his analysis of human life, he hated it. In effect, he says that whatever we do in life is worthless.

I do not agree with the speaker in **Ecclesiastes**. I do think that life has worth. But I do agree that many of the paths supposed to end in happiness do not. That, I believe, is worth thinking about.

To me, it seems significant that this great book was written long before the time of Christ. No doubt the writer could then truly say, 'There is no new thing under the sun.' After Christ came and lived and walked and taught among us, however, that could no longer be said.

As a teacher for almost forty years, I observed that most people make the really important decisions of their lives before they are twenty-five years old, some of them before they are fifteen. After that they live with those decisions for fifty years or so. When they get to the end, sometimes they feel their decisions have been wrong. Observers can shrug their shoulders and say, 'Too bad! _____didn't seem to know any better. Tough.'

But if you are a college student, or a junior or senior high student, sometimes you feel that you do not really have time to think things through. After all, you have counselors and programs and peers to advise you. Though it is true that most of them will not be around fifty years later to accept responsibility for any mistakes you make, you are likely to follow their advice. — Won't such advice bring you happiness?

In my opinion, the time to be cautious, to analyze carefully all that is advertised about happiness, is before you make those important decisions: what career to follow, what goals to give your heart to, what courses and college programs to take, even what person one should marry — or not marry.

Fortunately, however, there is often another chance. This fact, the fact of another chance, should not be relied on too heavily when one is young, for it is usually much simpler to make the best choice the first time. But the second chance is often there. Certainly this is true of choosing a career and of deciding what else is needed to provide happiness in life. As a college teacher, I saw many women and some men going back to college in their thirties and forties. Often they were preparing themselves to enter new careers. And I have known several people who have entered the professional Christian ministry in those years, though being a professional minister is not necessary to being a good Christian. Even in retirement, some folks embark on study programs in quite different fields, though many simply work out their own programs. (I knew a nurse who retired in her sixties, returned to college, and earned a degree with a major in history. The oldest student I ever had in my classes was a man of eighty-three, though I had quite a number in their fifties, sixties, and seventies.) An initial decision need not be a final decision, particularly if following the original one means a wasted life, a life of vanity and vexation of spirit.

CHAPTER THREE
Laws for Living
Deuteronomy 5:1-21

Everyone has heard of the Ten Commandments. Not everyone, however, knows what they are. Traditionally we say that God gave these commandments to Moses, the leader of the Jewish people in their flight from Egypt. They are first listed in the Old Testament in the book of **Exodus**, Chapter 20; here, in **Deuteronomy**, we are being reminded of what Moses did and said in the time described in **Exodus**.

The Ten Commandments do not constitute the whole of the Law which God gave the Jewish people to live by; but they are at the center of it, and all of us should be familiar with these ten major laws. (They are also referred to as the Decalogue, a word that uses the Latin word for ten, **Deca**, as the first part plus a word that sometimes means word, but sometimes means more than just a word.) The first five books of the Old Testament (**Genesis, Exodus, Leviticus, Numbers, and Deuteronomy**) are often referred to as The Law, the **Torah** in Hebrew; scholars also use the term **Pentateuch**, the first part of which means five in Greek.) Any reader knows that there are many narrative accounts in those first five books, as well as many laws, some major, like the Ten Commandments, and some very detailed. Yet these books are called The Law. The Jewish people regarded them as the most sacred of all the books of scripture.

It is probably necessary for most readers of scripture to know also that Jewish experts in the laws of Moses, scribes, developed hundreds, even thousands, of specific applications of the basic laws God had given to the Jewish people. There are occasions in New Testament incidents in which these additions by scribes are included in the word Law. Here, however, we are concerned only with the Ten Commandments.

The commandments are not numbered in the Bible, and major religious denominations number them somewhat differently. I use a numbering system that is common to Baptists, Methodists, Presbyterians, Disciples of Christ, and that is the numbering system that appears below. Jewish authorities regard verse 6 (in Deuteronomy 5) as the first Commandment, but Christian denominations begin with verse 7. Both Roman Catholics and Lutherans link what I have listed below as the first two commandments in the first commandment, then make the fourth commandment the third, the fifth commandment the fourth, and so on, dividing

17

what I have listed as the tenth commandment into two parts. The result, however, is the same, for the same laws are stated, only in a different numbering system.

Here they are:

1. **Thou shalt have no other gods before me.** Remembering how many idols were worshipped in ancient times by the neighbors of the Jewish people, we may at first think that this commandment has little to do with us today. On second thought, however, we may conclude that the temptation to do whatever our neighbors, or competitors, are doing in order to obtain the maximum amount of production is just as great today as it ever was. — Often we heed far more closely the slogan 'everybody does it' than any commandment in the bible.

2. **Thou shalt not make thee any graven image.** Some Protestant writer has suggested that a mother can worship her child. One Catholic catechism suggests that Marxism may become, or is, a form of idolatry; hence, the pic ture of a Communist leader may become an object of worship. Perhaps I have given my heart to the Buick in the garage, or to the house I live in. Some writers suggest that the currency is an object of worship, an engraved image. Some suggest that the national flag can become such an object. No matter what the technical definitions of the words may be, I feel that I and my generation are just as prone to breaking this commandment as any other generation ever was. That is my

3. **Thou shalt not take the name of the Lord thy God in vain.** A prayer that God may condemn someone to Hell is a common, everyday sort of curse. At least it seems to be, if one reads modern plays carefully: plays, novels, television scripts, film scripts. Quakers have traditionally felt that this commandment forbids taking an oath of of fice or an oath in court (supported further, some feel, by certain New Testament passages.) Some have even applied this commandment to a casual commitment to a church.

4. **Keep the Sabbath day to sanctify it.** As most Christians are supposed to know, the Jewish sabbath was on the last day of the week, Saturday; Christians made Sunday the sabbath because on that day Christ's resurrection took place. Most Christians now think of Sunday as the sabbath. Although many of us go to church on Sunday morning, not many of us seem to take seriously any restrictions on shopping on Sunday. That statement does not need either defense or illustration. Sometimes we think of the sabbath as a day of rest, with much scriptural support for this, but even what we do under the name of recreation is often not very resting. If a family today were to spend Sunday morning in church, Sunday evening in church, and most of Sunday afternoon in the study of the scriptures, that family would be likely to be in a tiny minority in most American communities. Yet those of us who are seventy, particularly those of us who were in Scotland during World War II, can remember when many com-

munities took this commandment very seriously. Perhaps they were wrong; I find it difficult to say that what we do now is better than what our grandparents did in the nineteenth century, however. I do not think that we have improved.

5. **Honor thy father and thy mother.** At some point in my own lifetime, 'authorities' -- whoever they are, decided that the younger generation should not trust anyone over thirty -- at a time when all the parents of that generation were over thirty Some findings of modern soft sciences such as sociology and psychology were applied to this and enough examples of poor parents were found and publicly criticized to cause a shift away from honoring parents, no matter how good they were. !- One can argue that public opinion of government officials, journalists, and the leaders of all professions and businesses has shifted away from respect and toward contempt in the same years. But candidates for office in all political parties now seem to regard 'family values' as a good thing. --We do not know what may happen. -- Some 'authorities' have suggested that to the degree we honor our parents we must accept their ideas. What we might better remember is that if we take the trouble to study the problems another generation has been through, we may be able to honor the members of that generation even though we ourselves feel it is better to use different methods. We might be less shocked when we ourselves discover later that we have made mistakes: that we are not perfect.

6. **Thou shalt not kill.** The original word here translated as kill meant murder, I am told. As we discover later, in what is called the Sermon on the Mount, Jesus tells us that we should not even be angry at other people, that, in fact, we should love our enemies. This is one of the commandments that we often seek to write into our laws, and in that process we often get into debates about such matters as capital punishment, abortion, war, and violence. For each of us there is a difficult challenge to be faced.

7. **Neither shalt thou commit adultery.** We all know what adultery is at least in a general way. We know that married couples are supposed to be loyal to each other, that the intimate marriage relationship becomes shaky indeed when the two parties to the relationship feel that they are unable to trust each other. In his analysis of this commandment, Jesus tells us that we should not have lust in our hearts for someone who is not our spouse. Being able to trust one other person completely is, many of us believe, one of the greatest benefits of marriage. Any act or thought that could be labeled a breach of trust could be considered a kind of adultery.

Some have held that this special loyalty between two human beings, the loyalty that occurs in a good marriage, teaches the marriage partners much about the meaning of being a Christian; for they learn the value of sacrifice for someone else, of putting the interests and needs of someone else ahead of our own selfish desires and needs. The love of a lifetime, which one develops in a good marriage, certainly helps each of us move beyond his or her own ego, a major step in understanding what it is to be a Christian.

One modern Catholic catechism analyzes this commandment along with the first part of what we here refer to as the tenth commandment: 'Thou shalt not covet thy neighbor's wife.' That certainly makes sense.

8. **Neither shalt thou steal.** The same Catholic catechism that links the commission of adultery with coveting one's neighbor's wife links stealing with coveting the neighbor's property. Again, such a linking makes sense.

It would also be possible to link this commandment with the ninth commandment whenever we apply the ninth to gossip. Shakespeare has told us that the theft of a reputation, a good name, is more serious than the theft of property. We might agree with Shakespeare, except that so many of us find it so much fun to gossip -- and seldom are we arrested because of what we have said privately about another human being.

As a retired English teacher, I discovered many years ago that I had expanded the definition of the word **steal** more than my students had. For example, one college student preparing to teach told me that it was all right for a student to cheat on a bad test (the student making the judgment of what was a bad test.) That was during the weird days of the late sixties, when college students were listening to all sorts of voices. But even in more civilized times students have found it difficult to understand why plagiarism could be considered stealing.

This commandment is not just about visible, tangible property, many of us feel. It is, like most of the commandments, first of all a state of heart and mind, an attitude that puts the self first, not God, not one's neighbor.

9. **Neither shalt thou bear false witness against thy neighbor.** Not many of us are called to testify in courts. If and when we are, however, we know that our system of laws permits the accused person to be confronted with his or her accusers and requires those accusers to be held accountable for the veracity of what they say, with penalties for false witness. To some degree, this commandment influenced the development of these laws governing court procedures.

Often when we think of this commandment, we think of gossip. Why not? Gossip violates all of the legal requirements for witnesses: The accused does not confront the accusers and is not given a chance to defend himself or herself. The accusers are not usually in any danger of punishment themselves for telling lies, even for presenting only one side of a case, the bad side.

One commentary even says that it is a sin if we tell the truth about someone repeatedly, if it is something bad.

10. Neither shalt thou desire thy neighbor's wife, neither shalt thou covet thy neighbor's house, his field, or his manservant, or his maidservant, his ox, or his ass, or anything that is thy neighbor's.

One commentary says that the tenth commandment sums up all of the ten, for one who covets, puts self before God or other people.

Often we find it convenient not to preach about this commandment and others and others that seem to contradict the slogans of the world outside the church. Perhaps that is why so many persons who go to church, who call themselves Christians, and who are proud to be on the side of morality, as they define it, at least, are not even aware of the ways in which many of these commandments, perhaps all, could be applied to themselves.

A personal view: Although I cheer for certain teams and have spent much time in getting ahead in the world, as we call it, I wonder if I have really considered the implications of the commandment against coveting. Isn't that a part of the reason why I bought a new car recently, and why I have retired in a house that is bigger than I really need? — What could possibly be my excuse, except to say that 'everybody else does it?'

— It would be good for each of us to refresh his or her memory now and then about the nature and implications of the ten commandments. There is much evidence that regular church members do not do that.

Sometimes we think of such laws as placing burdens on our shoulders. It surprises some of us to discover that many devout Jews were pleased that they had been given the Law, for the Law, first of all in these commandments, but also in other laws and rules in the Bible and elsewhere, gave the Jewish people a better way of living than their neighbors of other faiths had. Many of them actually felt blessed because God had given them a good way to live. — What a beautiful concept!

CHAPTER FOUR
THE LAW IN ESSENCE
Micah 6:8

It is not a tremendous task, even for an old man like me, to memorize the Ten Commandments, which we have discussed in the previous chapter. Some passages in scripture, however, have been said to summarize all ten; **Micah 6:8** is one of them.

In the King James translation, that verse reads: 'He hath shewed thee, O man, what is good; and what doth the Lord require of thee, but to do justly, and to love mercy, and to walk humbly with thy God?'

Those of us who believe that this summarizes the Ten Commandments point out that if we 'walk humbly' with our God, we shall not seek to put ourselves in God's place; instead, we shall worship God as our only God (and not worship ourselves), we shall not worship any graven images, and, because we are humble toward God, we shall not take His name in vain and, of course, we shall honor the day of each week dedicated especially to His worship. We also feel that doing justly and loving mercy will ensure that we do not kill, steal, bear false witness, or covet, with respect to our neighbors, and that we will show respect and honor to our parents.

A knowledge of the original Ten Commandments will help us to remember how this Bible verse summarizes their content. I believe, so I suggest, that each of us should commit to memory all of the Ten Commandments in addition to this verse from **Micah**.

Now how does the book of **Micah** fit into the Old Testament? We have said in an earlier chapter that **Ecclesiastes** is one of the books the Jews called writings, or sacred writings, and that the Jewish people considered these writings important to know about, but not on the same level as the Law and the Prophets. We have also said that to the Jewish people the first five books of the Bible were referred to as the Law, (Usually, but not quite always, when a New Testament reference is made to the Law, it means these five books.) Obviously, **Micah** is not one of the first five books of the Bible. To the Jews, the name 'former prophets' was applied to Old Testament books we often refer to as history: **Joshua, Judges, Samuel** (I and II, in our numbering), and **Kings** (again, I and II, to us.) We do not usually think of those books as the prophets, though the Jews did.

The Jews called the following books 'the latter prophets,' and they are the books we generally think of in that way, perhaps because all of them except **Jonah** are attributed to the writers and prophets whose names they bear: (**Jonah** is a book about the prophet, not writ ten by him.) **Isaiah, Jeremiah, Ezekiel,** and the book of the Twelve (The Jewish name for one book that included the last twelve books of the Old Testament in most English translations: **Hosea, Joel, Amos, Obadiah, Jonah, Micah, Nahum, Habakkuk, Zephaniah, Haggai, Zachariah, and Malachi.**) **Micah** is one of the twelve, which are also called the 'minor prophets', not because their words are of minor importance, but because the books are relatively short.

The Jewish religious leaders regarded as sacred both the former and the latter prophets.

A prophet was someone called by God to preach His word to His people. Frequently such a person prophesied what would happen to those people if they did not obey God, but our modern definition of the word that means one who predicts was not true of all of the utterances of a prophet; many of these were meant to interpret for the listeners the ways in which God's Law applied to their daily lives. The prophet, then, was, among other things, what we today would call a preacher.

In the chapter from which this verse is taken, the prophet Micah is speaking to a group of people who are probably somewhat like today's Americans, the prosperous ones, at least. It was the custom in their day to offer to God sacrifices of their possessions, often cattle and sheep, as burnt offerings. Some neighboring tribes had offered as sacrifices to the idols they worshipped, their firstborn, what would have been an extreme sacrifice, indeed. But Micah, the prophet, reminds the Jewish people that God does not want such a simple kind of sacrifice, however costly and inconvenient to themselves; God did not want to be propitiated — but to be obeyed! And obedience required that they treat others with justice and mercy and be humble (rather than proud) toward God; their pride in themselves and in everything they possessed (sometimes acquired by unjust and merciless means) would get in the way of being humble toward God.

It is easy to see why so many people know this verse by heart. It is a good reminder of what we often forget, the Ten Commandments. It is best, however, if we know the Ten.

Sometimes we become discouraged when we look at the institutional churches of our time and at the complacent, hypocritical persons within them. It can be even more discouraging to know that such hypocritical disobedience to God's commandments existed in Jewish societies thousands of years ago, and that they developed rather quickly in Christian churches, as well (See **Revelation**, chapters 1-3). On the other hand, it can also be encouraging to look at the pockmarked history of the church established by God. I find it encouraging. It is a reminder to me that never in the history of God's dealings with human beings have those human beings been able to be perfect. Beginning with that point of view, I can expect less of the church, demand more of myself, and be glad that the church does, after all, provide a place for me to meet with other sinners and, sometimes at least, be helped in my too feeble struggles to be obedient to God.

Yet we know that one of the principal reasons why those who remain outside the church do so is that they see how many hypocrites there are in the church and decide that the church is not worth joining. -- I believe that it is; I do not believe that I shall ever find a perfect church, however; nor do I believe that I shall ever achieve perfection in myself; hence, I can never consciously substitute myself for God.) The real danger of persons within the church is complacency; we may look at the rest of society and feel that in some respects we are morally superior to 'those people,' then rest on our laurels, as it were: decide that we do not need to look at our own sins any more and try to reform them. —- When we do that, we are truly in danger.

Not a great poem, but one that was written by a scholar who was turned off by the church of his time, as he viewed it from both within and without, was the Victorian British writer Arthur Hugh Clough's 'The Latest Decalogue.' (Remember that the word decalogue means ten commandments.) Clough was a good friend of Matthew Arnold, a better poet and an agnostic; one who, however, dismissed the Christianity in which he had been raised without giving it the careful consideration that his friend Clough did. Arnold's decisive dismissal of Christianity was not, one should point out, an indication of a superior intellect, for persons with intellects at least equal to Arnold's have since then found ways to justify what Arnold was repulsed by, repulsed or confused. But to Clough and others, the way church members lived in the prosperous Britain of his day was a major reason for doubt. As I have said, it should not have been.

25

Here is Clough's poem:

The Latest Decalogue

Thou shalt have one God only; who
Would be at the expense of two?
No graven image may be
Worshipped, except the currency;
Swear not at all; for by thy curse
Thine enemy is none the worse:
At church on Sunday to attend
Will serve to keep the world thy friend:
Honour thy parents; that is, all
From whom advancement may befall;
Thou shalt not kill; but need not strive
Officiously to keep alive:
Do not adultery commit;
Advantage rarely comes of it:
Thou shalt not steal; an empty feat,
When it's so lucrative to cheat;
Bear not false witness; let the lie
Have time on its own wings to fly:
Thou shalt not covet, but tradition
Approves all forms of competition.

CHAPTER FIVE
Comfort and Strength
Psalm 23

The Psalms are easy to find in most Bibles; Just open to about the middle, and there they are. They are so much treasured by Christians that copies of the New Testament, printed separately from the Old Testament, often add the Psalms as the only book from the Old.

They are sometimes called collectively the hymn book of the early Christian church. In many Bibles, one finds instructions for the musicians printed above certain psalms. They are poems, as the lyrics of hymns and other songs are, and some of them can be sung without alteration. In many of our modern hymnals there are hymns based on the psalms or Bible psalms slightly rearranged in meter to fit our traditional ideas of rhyming songs. In the Scottish Presbyterian churches in my own lifetime just such reworked psalm's were often used as a hymnal, I am told.

But it was not only a hymnal; it was also a prayer book. These prayers are often used in the various kinds of liturgies that appear in modern churches. **Some** of them are, I should add, for there are some psalms that have been listed as 'cursing psalms,' and cursing, we know, is not part of the Christian religion. — For many years, I was disturbed by those so-called cursing psalms; in my personal attempts to organize the Bible in a consistent manner (my personal theology, one might confess), I more or less put them out of my mind, perhaps as a mystery that I was not able yet to penetrate. Then I read the little book by C. S. Lewis on the psalms, and I could finally read all of them with sympathy, understanding, and, in most cases, with the admiration they deserved. At this point I shall not attempt to explain what Lewis said, only that I strongly recommend his book to anyone and that I believe it is good to withhold judgment on the book of 150 psalms until one has read Lewis. (I first knew C. S. Lewis's work because of his distinguished contributions to the body of English scholarship; only later did I discover his brilliant writing on Christianity.)

During the eight years when I regarded my visits to the elderly and to other shut-ins as my principal Christian service, I found that many of them were Bible readers and that their Bibles were often marked at certain psalms. In fact, the **Psalms** and portions of **Isaiah** were most frequently marked by the elderly I visited with. To these persons who had little left of material comfort, the psalms were a reminder that they retained one very great source of comfort, no matter how bad things were for them themselves; they could turn to God as a source of comfort and strength.

Psalm 23 is surely everyone's favorite. Often it is printed on the inside of the cover of funeral bulletins. Sometimes it is read aloud by all of those attending a funeral service. It is a prayer of praise to God, a reminder to the person praying that when human strength fails, God is still there, ready if it is best to help. With God, as Jesus tells us, all things are possible. — We do know, of course, that our prayer should not insist that God do exactly what we think is best, only that God's will be done. Many persons who pray, then, add the phrase 'if it be Thy will.' — As in the cursing psalms, we do not always pray for what is best; our egos may be too much involved.

Psalm 23:
'The Lord is my shepherd; I shall not want.
He maketh me to lie down in green pastures; he leadeth me beside the still waters.
He restoreth my soul; he leadeth me in the paths of righteousness for his name's sake.
Yea, though I walk through the valley of the shadow of death, I will fear no evil; for thou art with me; thy rod and thy staff they comfort me.
Thou preparest a table before me in the presence of mine enemies; thou anointest my head with oil; my cup runneth over.

Surely goodness and mercy shall follow me all the days of my life; and I will dwell in the house of the Lord forever.'

-- Those six verses have been memorized by millions.
They do not really need explanation, do they? — One might point out the fact that the early Hebrews knew a great deal about the care of sheep by their shepherds, and that the word **pastor** originally meant shepherd, but I think that this psalm speaks for itself. It does to me.

Above all, it seems to me, this psalm reminds its readers that there is some being greater, wiser, and stronger than any human being. Often we forget this; often we feel, even devout church members, that we ought to be able to meet any crisis on our own. Then there comes a time when we encounter a problem that we cannot handle without help; that brings us up short. How do we avoid depression and despair? We turn to God in prayer, and if our faith is strong enough, we can pray in such words as those of **Psalm 23**. This psalm is a prayer of affirmation, of trust in God, of confidence in the power of God to provide whatever is needed, no matter how difficult the crisis may be.

CHAPTER SIX
Human Disobedience and God's Mercy
Jonah

One of the Christians I most admire was C. S. Lewis, as I have suggested in the previous chapter. One of the reasons I admire him, I am sure, is that he was a college English teacher (Oxford and Cambridge) and had what I regard as an English teachers way of reading God's scriptures, looking through and past the details to see what God is saying to human minds, minds that are easily distracted by details and that try so hard so often to be substitutes for God's mind.— I say all of this because the book of **Jonah** is one of my favorites. I am sure, however, that my interpretation of that book will not be the same as any official interpretation promulgated by Catholic, Mainline Protestant, or Conservative Protestant spokespersons. Not exactly, anyhow. I read it as an English teacher would -- at least, as I read other materials when I was an English teacher. Please forgive me for this, and be sure to ask whatever priest or pastor you finally choose for that person's (or that denomination's) interpretation of **Jonah**.

The man Jonah was a prophet; hence, he was committed to the service of God. It was his job to do what God told him to do, to obey God.

In the opening passage, we find God speaking to Jonah and telling him what to do, what God wanted him to do:

'Now the word of the Lord came unto Jonah the son of Amittai, saying:

Arise, go to Nineveh, that great city, and cry against it; for their wickedness is come up before me.'

As an English teacher who has also been active in churches for most of his life, I identify with Jonah.

It is true that, as a Protestant, I have about the same responsibility as Jonah, since he was a prophet and I am a member of a church that accepts the traditional belief in the priesthood of all believers. But I believe that Catholics can also identify with the prophet Jonah, most of them at least, even some of the priests who have taken vows of obedience.

Jonah has evidently received the blessings of God, the knowledge of the kinds of laws and habits of living that are most likely to bring happiness. In one sense, we can say that Jonah's selfish interests have been taken care of by God. Just as ours have; most of them.

Does Jonah do what we would probably do? Of course:

'But Jonah rose up to flee unto Tarshish from the presence of the Lord, and went down to Joppa; and he found a ship going to Tarshish: so he paid the fare thereof, and went down into it, to go with them unto Tarshish from the presence of the Lord.'

Such disobedience may sound incredible to one who seeks Christian meaning for life as I hope you do. Remember, actually living as a Christian requires of each of us obedience to God. And God does not always tell us to do what is pleasant and comfortable; sometimes He tells us that we, the members of churches, should do something about the problems of those great cities in our own society: the cities where drug dealers keep defenseless people in fear of their lives, where gang organizations flourish, and where the churches have left, many of them.

But Nineveh is not only a great city of many human souls. Even worse, it is in a land that has been hostile to Israel. If Jonah were to go there to preach, he would be taking risks. More important for him, Jonah would have to overcome his hate for the people of that country! How else could he serve them? How else could he treat them as human beings with souls that deserved saving?

As we would probably do, those of us who go to church in America today, Jonah tries to run away. Nineveh is in the east, Tarshish in the west. Jonah takes ship for Tarshish.

We all remember the next part of the story. Jonah is cast overboard and is swallowed by a big fish.

At this point, I reveal my English teacher background, for I am less absorbed in the details than in the main point of the story. I do not find it necessary to get out a pair of calipers and measure the mouths of fish to find out whether or not any fish is large enough to swallow a human being whole. —Although I have been told that such a large fish can be found, that is not the point. After finding himself in the depths of hopeless despair, unable to save himself by his own efforts, Jonah prays to God for help. He promises to be obedient this time, if God will only give him another chance.

God saves him.

So grudgingly Jonah goes to Nineveh and preaches against its sins. -- Some commentators suggest that the story of his miraculous rescue from the fish has preceded him to Nineveh and that the people there are convinced that Jonah is truly under God's guidance. That would make sense, of course. But for whatever reason, the people of Nineveh, all social classes, repent.

After they repent, God shows mercy on them and chooses not to destroy the city after all.

So far, then, the story of Jonah is about the results of disobedience and obedience and in the case of Nineveh, of sin and repentance. But there is another point at the end of the story.

A plant that has given Jonah shade becomes withered and dies. Jonah, still hating Nineveh, never having forgiven the people there and accepted them as fellow human beings, becomes angry, first at God's mercy for Nineveh, then because God permits the plant to die.

God points out Jonah's problem.

We can see ourselves in every action Jonah takes.

The story of Jonah is about a good person, someone like us. We can learn much from it.

NOTE ON THE TWO TESTAMENTS OF THE BIBLE

How much of the Old Testament a Christian should use, and in what way, depends a good deal on the particular branch of the Christian Church the reader chooses to unite with. Some of my own personal favorite passages in the Old Testament have been omitted in the preceding pages, for my purpose has been simply to offer a sampling of what may be found in those books that comprise the bulk of our Bible and that served as the scriptures for the early Christians.

Those Christian churches that place much emphasis on liturgy (Catholic, Episcopal, Lutheran, and Eastern Orthodox) derive much of their ritual from the Old Testament, though tradition since the time of Christ has altered the ritual a great deal. In each of these denominations, the role of the priest, or of the priest substitute, is important, whatever Luther and his early followers may have said about the priesthood of all believers.

31

Most Christian churches look to the Old Testament for predictions and descriptions of the Messiah to come (**Isaiah**, for example, is much quoted.)

In His own preaching, Jesus often cited Old Testament passages, as footnotes in many Bibles indicate.

But after a period in which specifically Christian preachings were shared orally by the early Christian churches, various individuals recorded in writing the Christian message. Those records make up what we call the New Testament.

CHAPTER SEVEN
The Temptations of Christ
Matthew 4:1-11

Not everyone is comfortable in dealing with references to the devil. I am. Some readers take the term literally, others as a symbol for a human propensity for doing the wrong thing. But I have seen enough of evil in myself and in the world to believe that there is some force at work in human life that causes us to find sin more attractive than goodness. If you have problems with the word **devil**, you may find it easier to read this term as self-centeredness or selfishness; those words will work about as well. I do not need a substitute.

After having been in a wilderness for many days, one would naturally be hungry. Jesus was. The devil reminded Him that he could use His holy powers to provide comfort for Himself. He could turn stones into bread. But Jesus told the tempter, 'Man shall not live by bread alone, but by every word that proceedeth out of the mouth of God.'

Interpreters argue over the meaning of this passage. A Catholic commentary says that all three temptations are to misuse holy power. A Methodist commentary from the 1920's says that this particular temptation is for the member of the clergy to take time away from his teaching and preaching mission to do such social work as feeding the poor. It might also be taken, in my opinion, to refer to the desire all human beings have for comfort. For example, we seem more willing to pay for cushioned seats in church than for missions to the inner city. Even some pastors, no doubt concerned about the welfare of their families, place pastoral salaries and benefits first in the church budget process. -- I do not mean by this that most pastors are overpaid, only that the temptation to be as comfortable as those of us in the pews is sometimes there, taking precedence over their spiritual mission in life.

In the second temptation, Jesus is taken to the pinnacle of the temple and told to throw Himself down from it, relying on supernatural power to save Him from death. -- Most interpreters take this to mean that the miraculous rescue from death will bring in crowds to hear Jesus, since the miracle will be a sign of His divinity. And we do not need to describe in detail the television preachers and others who have sometimes been prone to the use of such tricks to bring in the crowds. Some would say that Elmer Gantry's famous Sunday evening shows were of this sort. Others might argue in reply that a hired performer, musical or instrumental or whatever, would fit the second temptation, whether the performer is of rock or jazz or classical nature. — Whatever the case, Jesus chose **not** to use this method; in fact, later, when he performed miracles of healing, he repeatedly told those healed to tell no one. Evidently he wanted crowds to follow Him to hear the message of how to find divine happiness. Jesus had a mission, and he wished to complete that mission, so far as we can tell, in a straightforward way, with no spectacles to distract the people from the principal message.

Then we come to a temptation that seems to be very controversial today in its interpretation. We are told:

'Again, the devil taketh him up unto an exceeding high mountain, and showeth him all the kingdoms of the world, and the glory of them;

And saith unto him, All these things will I give thee, if thou wilt fall down and worship me.'

We ask ourselves at this point what the temptation is. With what is the devil tempting Jesus? — It is difficult not to think of the last days of Jesus on this earth, the final days before His crucifixion: We remember His triumphal entry into Jerusalem on the Sunday before the crucifixion, how the crowds came out and cheered His entry. We remember also what they expected the Messiah to do: to restore the Jewish people to political power. Some have even suggested that Judas Iscariot was one of those who expected Jesus to be that kind of Messiah, a political figure; and when Jesus was not, Judas betrayed Him. — But that we do not know. We only know what many of the Jewish people expected in their Messiah, a political and military leader, and that Jesus chose not to be that type.

Now would this temptation still apply today? The answer is controversial. In my opinion, it would, though many fine Christians disagree with my conclusion. They argue that it is necessary for pastors to lead their people into local and national government problems in order to persuade elected governing bodies to take action, sometimes on specific issues, sometimes on overall programs of reform.

My major argument against this is that only the members of the clergy are especially trained in religion and equipped to teach religion; if they leave their religious duties in order to go into politics, no one else will do what they are trained to do. I personally believe that this is why Jesus very firmly rejected the temptation to go into politics. It would have kept Him from doing what He was here to do.

We can say that Jesus had a ministry of only three years and that surely a modern pastor with more years at his or her disposal should be able to take out some time for political efforts. — Here, one problem is that the typical modern pastor has a job that requires more hours per week than any other profession does, as far as I know. I have interviewed twenty pastors in depth and have discovered that the sixty-hour week is the standard; some work many more hours than that. My own experience in business, teaching, government, and the professional ministry tells me that the total of sixty hours per week is too much. It does not leave enough, time for family, for personal refreshment and recreation, for study, and for prayer. — Some of the ministers I interviewed told me that they were embarrassed that they had so little time left over for their prayer lives. Yet we know that Jesus regularly left His disciples for a time to pray; prayer is essential for any spiritual leader.

As it is, the job of the church is seldom done as well as it should be done. Most pastors, and most church leaders, are conscientious; they want to do a good job. Yet the one way they see to doing that job is to do pretty much what other people are doing in their churches. Unfortunately, we have all neglected in the churches many matters of great importance. To name only two that I know a good deal about: Our Christian education programs are very poor indeed; and we seldom have adequate programs for taking the church to the elderly and other shut-ins. — Those are just local church matters; we can probably blame much of the crime in the cities on the fact that so many churches have left for the pleasanter suburbs and that few outlying churches have given much money and support to missions inside the high-crime areas. (Some have, I know, and they have been successful; but what a pitiful few.) — That is my basic argument against having the pastor of a church go into politics. I have many others, having been involved in politics myself (though not as a pastor), but in this respect, I believe that I see why Jesus decided not to seek political power.

The key of the Christian message follows, in what we call the Sermon on the Mount, **Matthew** 5, 6, and 7.

CHAPTER EIGHT
Christ's Sermon on the Mount
Matthew 5, 6, 7

It would be good to commit these three chapters of **Matthew** to memory. They represent the core of the Christian message in the opinion of many Christians. Generally we refer to these three chapters as the Sermon on the Mount.

The Happy People

The first twelve chapters of **Matthew** are called the Beatitudes; they tell us what kinds of people are truly blessed. But I like the translation of J. B Phillips, which uses the word **happy** instead of the word **blessed**. We are shocked at seeing the word **happy** used, but in part because we generally associate happiness with the achieve ment of worldly goals, the usual worldly goals: pleasure, power, money, status, self-development. Phillips explains somewhere that the Greek word meant happy in the way that the Greek gods of mythology were happy. Christians, instead of ancient Greeks, could still use the term if they were simply to think the modifier **spiritually** before each use of the word **happy.**

Some of the people I have known who have been most happy spiritually have had little wealth, power, or position. They have not been aggressive or assertive; they have not gone through life with chips on their shoulders, challenging everything and everybody. Instead, they have been people to whom such words as **meek, poor in spirit, merciful, peacemakers, pure in heart,** and the rest can be applied.

One may have difficulty imagining that a person who mourns is spiritually happy, but I have known mourners who for the first time in their lives were taking time to reflect on the meaning of life. In that meditation, I truly believe those mourners found a special, higher kind of happiness; one need not dismiss ice cream cones as without value in order to know that there is something a bit higher than the happiness eating ice cream represents. — Perhaps it is not out of place for me to add that, at seventy-one, I can no longer consume certain foods that once gave me great delight (those cooked in barbecue sauce and other hot spices); I cannot even eat a large steak or prime rib without some discomfort. On the other hand, I believe that I have as much happiness as I have ever had.

This passage opens our minds to some kinds of happiness that we may never have thought possible, too. Look at the rewards promised:

'Blessed are the poor in spirit: for theirs is the kingdom of heaven.

Blessed are they that mourn: for they shall be comforted.

Blessed are the meek: for they shall inherit the earth.

Blessed are they which do hunger and thirst after righteousness: for they shall be filled.

Blessed are the merciful: for they shall obtain mercy.

Blessed are the pure in heart: for they shall see God.

There is more, as you can read for yourself. But I believe that that is a fine place to stop. What greater happiness could there be than to 'see God'? I have known spiritually happy people who have truly seen God, have lived in His presence, and have known a kind of happiness that has been far finer than the kind I have had from eating an ice cream cone, pleasant as those cones have been.

Showing the Christian Way

First, then, Jesus tells us how to find real happiness: in directions never considered by the street-wise advisers who are all about us.

Then He tells us that we should live those lives in the sight of other people. Why? To show them the way, the better way.

In this passage and elsewhere, Jesus reminds us that the Pharisees have missed the point: They have done such things as fast and give alms and pray in order to be applauded by other human beings. — How foolish would seem to us the actions of the Pharisees; yet how often our own actions are intended to win the applause of humanity. Just as we cannot hide from God, we do not need to put on a show of how good we are for God; He already knows whether or not we are good. — Evidently this idea is hard for us to grasp. It is one thing to live our lives of spiritual happiness in such a way that those around us will want to live the same kinds of lives. It is quite another thing, however, to show off before to show off before other people. — How can we explain? It has to do with the

37

ego, I believe: In the first case, we remain humble and give any credit to God; in the second case, we are proud of what **we** have done. The difference is subtle, but it is there. The really happy people I have known have retained their humility. - This is a subject for genuine meditation; perhaps I cannot explain it.

The Law in Our Hearts

Can you obey the Ten Commandments, other wise go about business as usual, and feel proud of yourself — as some of the religious leaders of the Jews did in the time of Jesus? The answer, Jesus says, is no. (I realize, of course, that there were many special laws besides the Ten Commandments, but these were the most important, as Jesus frequently indicated.)

What is required, Jesus says, is for the commandments to take over our hearts, our attitudes toward all of life: Not only should we not kill, we should not be angry with our brother without a cause; not only should we not commit adultery, but we should not have lust in our hearts for a woman; finally, not only should we love our friends, but we should even love our enemies! This last statement (**Mat. 5:44**) is one of the most shocking in the New Testament; it says much of what Paul says in I **Corinthians 13:2**.

Once more, we are reminded that doing good things is not enough; our love for God should remind us that it is that love — and God's help — that makes it possible for us to do good. Whatever good we do is the result of our turning our lives over to the guidance of the Holy Spirit, not whatever human strength and will we can exert.

I know that old men have a habit of talking too much and that I have it to excess; yet I wish to tell a story il lustrating why many theologians have considered pride in self to be the worst sin of all. (Milton gives that sin to Satan, for example, in **Paradise Lost**.)

Soon after I was widowed, I investigated possibilities for Christian service, as my late wife and I had agreed I should do if she were to die. I needed one more year in the Minnesota teaching program in order to qualify for a retirement pension, so I asked for a part-time assignment as a preacher to test my potential in that direction. The only parish available was what is called a 'three-point charge,' one involving three small churches scattered over more than twenty miles. It had previously been a full-time assignment in the Methodist church, but the bishop had been unable to persuade any young seminary graduate to take it because the old parsonage was really not suitable for a young couple starting life out of college. I remained at home, forty miles away, taught a full schedule, and gave all of my weekends to the parish. It was good for me, for I soon discovered the great wisdom of that startling paradox stated in **Matthew 11:28-30**.

'Come unto me all ye that labour and are heavy laden, and I will give you rest.

Take my yoke upon you, and learn of me; for I am meek and lowly in heart; and ye shall find rest unto your souls.

For my yoke is easy, and my burden is light.

I discovered this, for I permitted myself to be led by the Holy Spirit within me. I was fully committed to serve Christ.

That year, we felt guided by the spirit of Christ to build a new parsonage and sell the old one. After we did, there was no problem in persuading a fine young married pastor to move into that parsonage; he stayed there long enough to build up the parish and make sure that it was once again what it had once been.

— But I was telling about myself and what happened to me. Naturally, we were all pleased at our overall success: building a new parsonage (and paying for it), having three seminary grads (or about-to-be) preach in the parish, having the parish people choose the one they wanted from the group, and so on.

My problem was a subtle one: I started out thinking that it was wonderful, what God had done; slowly I shifted to thinking how wonderful it was, what **we** had done; finally, after much praise from the fine people saying farewell to me, I started thinking how wonderful, what **I** had done! And that was the way I moved into my new parish, a quite different sort of parish, some two hundred miles away.

In the new parish, I worked hard, but I did so thinking that I had just shown that **I could** overcome any obstacle, do anything, no matter how difficult it was, no matter how many pastors had failed to do this in the ten years or so before my arrival. Not only did I not seek God's help; I did not even establish the best possible working relationships with the members of the tiny church I served as a full-time pastor.

At the end of the time allowed by my university to decide whether my leave was to become permanent or not, I knew that I had failed. Not even a spectacular failure. I had just been no more successful than my predecessors. Only a year or two later did it reach my understanding what had happened: I had left God out of the success plan, and I had lost my humility.

Now, in the Sermon on the Mount, Jesus was talking to people like me, like the man I was when I became proud of what I had accomplished.

It is not enough, Jesus tells us, here and elsewhere, to obey the Ten Commandments, technically at least, and to give back to God a percentage of what we have from Him as income. God wants us to commit ourselves completely.

We are to keep God's purposes first in our lives; whatever we need will be taken care of.

And just in case we start feeling proud — so easy to do after we have been used by God to ac complish something or after we have looked around ourselves at the weakness of other people's efforts, if any, to follow God — Jesus tells us: 'Be ye therefore perfect, even as your Father which is in heaven is perfect.' (5:48.) — I know that some interpreters suggest that we can actually achieve perfection in this life; my own interpretation, which may well be wrong, is that none of us should accept as a goal simply doing more than our neighbors; our goal should always be perfection, with a close scrutiny of our own faults to guide us, even though to know that perfection is impossible. Such a goal should keep us humble.

Don't Seek Human Praise

Not counting diplomas, I have nine framed certificates or plaques on my walls. One person I know has more than twenty. When I was a professor, I submitted to commit tees considering me as an applicant for a grant or special honor a several-page list of professional publications and presentations at programs; I also listed offices held previously in professional organizations and so on. Each quarter I distributed to my students evaluation sheets; sometimes I submitted them to department or college committees so that they could be considered as part of some total evaluation pro cess We treasure such things: What other people say about us, either officially or in private.

Jesus tells us, however, that we should not act to obtain the praise of other people. What we do is for God to evaluate. No one else, of course, really knows the truth; only God. Even we ourselves are not good judges of our own merits.

But we do get into the habit of living and acting for the praise of other people. Jesus knew this. He must have known how hard it is for us to break that habit. Obviously, with those certificates on my study walls, I must find it hard to break the habit.

But Jesus asks us to break a great many habits, including the ways in which we have previously looked at the world around us and determined the importance of what we see. Breaking habits is difficult. But first we have to identify those habits and determine to break them; that determination must come first.

Don't Judge Others

'Judge not, that you be not judged.' (7:1) How difficult that demand is! We really enjoy judging others, don't we?

Then whom should we judge? Ourselves! — That's no fun! — So how can we be surprised when we find that other people slip back into the habit of judging us, of gossiping? — We cannot really control those other people, can we? But we can find something to do ourselves, knowing that gossip is forbidden by God. Around every church and every community there is much good that can be done, good that should be done by someone, but which has been left without attention by anyone. There is always something better to substitute for gossip. We just have to look.

But first we have to decide that we can live without gossip. — This is important, for Jesus forbade it in His most famous sermon.

The Best Foundation

The Sermon on the Mount concludes with Jesus' famous narrative of the two builders: one who built on a solid foundation, the other who built on the sand. When storms came, the first one, built upon rock, remained standing; but the second one fell.

This part of the Sermon on the Mount is so familiar to all of us that it needs no explanation. We know that those who have heard or read these sayings and have used them to guide their lives have built on the foundation that Jesus calls solid, a rock. (Later Jesus will announce that He is building His church on a rock.)

Not all of the advice of Jesus for living our lives according to His teachings can be found in these three chapters of **Matthew**. But those chapters do contain the core of Christian belief. It would be good to read them over and over, returning to them regularly after we begin our church lives.

CHAPTER NINE
Following Christ
Luke 10:25-42

In selecting passages to illustrate the essence of the Christian message, I have had to omit many favorite passages. In this case, I wished to use one of the great and famous parables through which Jesus so often expressed the truths that cannot be stated in abstract terms, the narrative of The Good Samaritan. — Even though you have heard or read it before, I ask that you read it again. — The passage takes part of its meaning from the introduction, of course, which I have included. But when I was about to stop with verse 37, I noticed what followed, and, thinking of my long and often time wasting experiences in doing what institutional churches have told me was 'church work,' I felt that it was important that the last five verses of the chapter be included. — This may explain an otherwise quixotic inclusion.

In verse 25, the person described as a lawyer is, of course, an expert in the laws of Moses; today we might find someone similar on a seminary faculty. He is an expert, one who knows the right words, at least, for when Jesus asks him to give the answer written in the laws, the answer to the question, 'What shall I do to inherit eternal life?' he says:

'Thou shalt love the Lord thy God with all thy heart, and with all thy soul, and with all thy strength, and with all thy mind; and thy neighbor as thyself.'

Jesus then says, 'Thou hast answered right; this do, and thou shalt live.'

Before we examine the lawyer's next question, we should remember that his answer has been one of the summaries of the Ten Commandments. — We found one in the sixth chapter of **Micah**, as you may remember. —The first part of the answer summarizes the first four commandments, our loving duty to God; the last part, almost tossed off, it seems, summarizes our loving duty to our neighbors.

Then the lawyer (usually called a scribe) asks Jesus, 'Who is my neighbor?' The answer Jesus gives is in the form of that great parable.

As I read the parable now, I notice immediately that the priest and the Levite, who pass by on the other side of the road from the man who is in trouble, are religious persons, both of them. Perhaps because I have been an English teacher,

I translate the situation into modern terms, almost automatically. In those modern terms, I see two men conscious of their religious obligations, probably intent on being prompt in them — two men who are on their way to a church board meeting!

Of course they were not!

After all, this is the first century A. D. — But if they were not going to a church board meeting, they must have been intent on meeting some other religious obligation imposed by religious authorities for their time.

We live in a different century, but we are still the same kind of people, even religious people like me.

Another personal confession: In the early 1960's, I was very much involved in my 'church work' in southern California, first as an elder in a large Presbyterian church there, the clerk of session (church secretary for official purposes) for two years, next as the volunteer fund-raiser for a new sanctuary building at the church. Boy, was I ever religious! — In fact, though my wife helped me, by taking over the problems of our four growing children and by assisting in the fund-raising campaign, and though my four kids did mainly what four kids their age should do, particularly around the church, I did not take the time to do what I should have done as a father; I should have become a companion to them, particularly to the boys — something it was not fair to leave to my wife, and I should have done for them what I was already doing for the students in my classes. — At this point, I should not go into details, for the kids all turned out better than I might have expected them to. But one of them, in particular, perhaps all of them, needed my fatherly help through some pretty tough times. — It is never easy to be an adolescent, particularly when the father is too busy to help. — Now, I can't really blame the church, for much of it was my own ego, driving me to accomplish, to achieve. — Now I know what I did wrong. I also know that board meetings are not a good substitute for helping one's neighbor. Nowadays, we put our elderly parents in nursing homes, where someone else can care for them.

Nowadays, too, we have government programs to provide official charity for all kinds of people in distress. — Oh, now and then, when the home of someone in the community is destroyed by fire or when some similar disaster occurs, we rally around, take up a collection, even give up the time we normally spend on golf, water sports, and other hobbies, and do the neighborly thing. Not often, though.

But turning most things over to the government is really a cop-out, isn't it? We can sit in comfortable, air-conditioned board rooms in church and pass resolutions about what the government ought to do, then leave for the church supper and put on extra pounds. Can't we? —What a perfect solution to our problems: Have a meeting, pass a resolution, feel good and noble, and then dismiss to overindulge ourselves. — That is all a great deal easier than actually visiting the sick and the lonely in our own community, our own church even, and helping them with a portion of our own funds, helping them directly.

Incidentally, what we miss by not doing these things ourselves is a very precious kind of happiness, one that comes from helping others. If I had done this when I was forty, and taken my kids along when ever possible, we would all have been better for it.

But the Good Samaritan seems to have made helping other people, his neighbors, a regular part of his life. When Jesus asks the lawyer himself to decide which of these was a neighbor, he makes the right choice.

As you may know, the Samaritans were shunned by religious Jews; their theology was not quite right. That situation I am also inclined to apply to modern times, having been an English teacher.

Studying or Cooking?

The story of Mary and Martha is related to the story of the Good Samaritan because it is about 'church work.'

Jesus does not say that it is never necessary for anyone to be a hostess. He does tell Martha, however, that she worries about too many details and that the important thing is to seek Christian meaning for life, a meaning we know from the parable of the Good Samaritan that will be translated into action, Christian action.

Many years ago, I thought about writing an article on how I got the window screens painted; I was working on an M. A. then, I believe, and if given a choice between two obligations — painting the screens or studying —I found it easier to paint the screens. Around a church it is also easier to paint the screens, paint the walls, discuss the purchase of a new snowblower or lawnmower, or talk about what the government or someone else ought to do about a problem — much easier than studying and thinking about the Bible. — The adult classes at our church had one student in each class, the teacher; the rest were there to sit back and either listen or exchange greetings with one another or daydream. Church members seldom study much after the age of fourteen, an age when no one is ready to take on the huge abstractions involved in the study of religion. Although we have many beautiful Christian education buildings — along with the beautiful kitchens — in American churches, not one that I have seen would match even an undergraduate college in either the quality of its teaching staff or the requirements for students to complete courses.

Let me illustrate:

I live in a town of twenty thousand. There is a state university in our community, and in the Presbyterian church I attend, there are fourteen college faculty members, active or retired, in addition to six or seven with teaching certificates for public school work, college graduates in nursing, law, accounting, and the like. We have only two hundred or so church members. Other churches in town probably do not have such a high percentage of academic types, but they do have them. Our twin city, ten miles away, has another twenty thousand people and many college graduates in the churches. — About five years ago, I submitted to the chairperson of Christian education at our church a proposal for series of local courses offered for a full seminary credit by a seminary two hours away, a seminary that had agreed to cooperate.

At first, the Christian education committee did not even bother discussing the proposal.

After I asked them to, they did. Their conclusion: Worthless. They could not possibly develop a class of twenty-five adults, even including the members of other mainline churches in the two communities. — We are currently involved in a major fundraising effort to raise a hundred thousand dollars for building repair, and our church kitchen operates several times in a typical week. What Jesus had to say to Martha was important.

CHAPTER TEN
God's Mercy and Human Mercy
Luke 15

The core of chapter 15 of Luke is what we call the story of the Prodigal Son. Often we read it just that way, nod our proud heads, and say, 'See. God does have mercy on those who fall away and return.'

And that story is there, too. It is also easy to forget that. The Prodigal is what we today would call quite adolescent in his attitude toward life. He takes money that is not yet due him, goes away somewhere, where no one will know him, and really kicks up his heels. As for the money, he blows it! Then, his money gone and down on his luck, he starts feeling sorry for himself. He certainly doesn't deserve to be taken back, not after the childish way he has acted but he goes back anyhow, figuring that even his dad's servants lived more comfortably than he has been lately.

Not only does his father take him back, he has a feast of welcome for him, treats him well, and shows him all the love and mercy that no reasonable person would expect him to show.

'Reasonable person?' Yes. We know how the world works, and how it did even in those days. But this father, the Prodigal's father, is unreasonable, unreasonably merciful, unreasonable in his love for the Prodigal who has repented and come home.

In fact, this father is so merciful and loving that we think of him as being much like God Himself. Many of us think that in this parable the father stands for God.

But that is just the story of the younger son, the Prodigal. When Jesus begins the story, He says, 'A certain man had two sons.' We also need to know what happened to the older son.

After the father tells him joyfully that the younger brother has returned and that they are going to celebrate, the elder brother becomes angry and says, 'Lo, these many years do I serve thee, neither transgressed I at any time thy commandment: and yet thou never gavest me a kid, that I might make merry with my friends but as soon as this thy son was come, which hath devoured thy living with harlots, thou hast killed for him the fatted calf.'

We know the rest, of course, the father's explanation to his streetwise older son, his explanation about how life really ought to work and what is important in life.

We know.

The trouble is, we who go to church all the time still act the way the elder brother did. — Maybe we even say that it is just to do that: our human idea of justice. State university in our community, and in the Presbyterian church I attend, there are fourteen college faculty members, active or retired, in addition to six or seven with teaching certificates for public school work, college graduates in nursing, law, accounting, and the like. We have only two hundred or so church members. Other churches in town probably do not have such a high percentage of academic types, but they do have them. Our twin city, ten miles away, has another twenty thousand people and many college graduates in the churches. — About five years ago, I submitted to the chairperson of Christian education at our church a proposal for a series of local courses offered for full seminary credit by a seminary two hours away, a seminary that had agreed to cooperate.

At first, the Christian education committee did not even bother discussing the proposal.

After I asked them to, they did. Their conclusion: Worthless. They could not possibly develop a class of twenty-five adults, even including the members of other mainline churches in the two communities. — We are currently involved in a major fundraising effort to raise a hundred thousand dollars for building repair, and our church kitchen operates several times in a typical week. What Jesus had to say to Martha was important.

But the father, like God, says that the younger son was dead; now he is alive again.

The problem with understanding this parable is that we may apply it to other people, not to ourselves.

If nothing else, this parable should make it clear to all of us that we do not have the mind of God, that our ideas of what should be reasonable are not the same as God's.

The human mind does not work as God's does. Our minds are more like that of the elder brother in this great parable. We can see this when we analyze people around us but not when we look at ourselves.

CHAPTER ELEVEN
The Incarnation
John 3:16 ; Mark 14-16

There are three positions taken by most Christians that any 'outsider' must come to terms with before becoming a fully committed Christian:

First, that God exists, a Being generally identifiable with what may be found in the Bible.

Second, that 'God so loved the world that he gave his only begotten Son, that whosoever believeth in him should not perish, but have everlasting life.' (**John 3:16**).

Third, that God can work miracles. — It would be foolish indeed to suppose that any one of these is easy to accept. But neither is the opposite.

As to the first, the existence of God, I would suggest that you ask pastors whom you are considering as potentially your pastor to explain it to you. (By pastor, I include Catholic priests, mainline Protestant pastors, and Conservative Protestant pastors.) — Because all pastors are very busy people, Protestants as well as Catholics, you should phone the pastor's office first, tell the pastor what you wish to talk about, so she or he can be prepared, then be prompt and courteous in getting the answer to your question, the answer that that pastor has to offer. Not only will you discover whether the pastor has a clear idea about how to answer your question, but you will also find out a good deal about the pastor herself or himself. But do not waste time. Do plan to study carefully whatever materials the pastor may give you or recommend to you, and show your appreciation for the time the pastor gives to you.

Incidentally — if that is an appropriate word here — I do believe in God, God as found in the Bible. I know of many men and women smarter than I am who do not; but I also know of many — at least as many — who are just as smart as the others and who do. The answer you seek is not one determined by the degree of your intelligence; of that, I am quite sure.

As to the possibility of miracles, you may find many books on this subject. Those books often say what needs to be said better than I could say it and much more completely than we have space for in this book. For my own part, the belief in God, which I have, makes possible any miracle that could be performed by

God. I have never worshipped science as a god, certainly not what I call the soft sciences, so I find no conflict between believing in God and believing in some other kind of god, such as 'scientific man,' for example. All through my life I have been witness to miracles of one sort or another, one of the greatest of these, to me, has been seeing a selfish human being become unselfish. Enough said.

The Incarnation, as we call it, is, of course, the greatest miracle of them all.

As most Christians believe, God created the world and repeatedly told the created human beings what they must do, giving them freedom either to obey or to disobey. Over and over God's chosen people disobeyed His laws. Finally, God sent His Son, Jesus, the Christ, to live out as well as teach what human beings should do and be. The very people whom God had spoken to before, His chosen people, rejected Jesus as the Messiah (or Christ), thinking that the Messiah would be a military and political leader like King David. They put Jesus as the Messiah (or Christ), thinking that the Messiah would be a military and political leader like King David. They put Jesus to death on the cross. Jesus was resurrected, however, and appeared to many of those who had formerly followed Him. His resurrection was a sign that all who believed in Him and did His will would also have eternal life.

All of this is stated in **John 3:16**, probably the most-often memorized verse in the Bible. It sums up what many Christian interpreters identify as the single most important fact of their belief. We believe that God became flesh and dwelt among us, that He showed us the way to happiness — a way that contradicts what the world outside the Christian church recommends, and that after living a model life on this earth, He was resurrected from the dead.

Now that is undoubtedly a difficult concept to accept. Many millions do; other millions have. The four Gospels (**Matthew, Mark, Luke, and John**) testify to the truth of this improbable statement. Within three hundred years, the Christians who had known Jesus and their successors had officially converted the Roman Empire. They had done so because the teachings of Jesus made more sense than did the alternatives: power, violence, hate, mean spiritness, and the like (what we sometimes call 'street wisdom' to day.) Whether or not it was good that the Roman Empire was officially converted is another matter; Christianity, through the testimony of the followers of Jesus and their heirs, was so indomitable that the mighty Empire had little choice but to compromise with the Christians.

Many Christians today turn to the powerful testimony of the four Gospels for proof of what happened. But for whatever reason, many of us believe that God lov ed the world He had created and that He still does. By becoming flesh and dwelling among us, He showed us the way to live and to be happy, truly happy.

Like the Jewish people of ancient times, we often close our ears and eyes to what God has told us and has shown us we should do.

Mark 14-16

I shall not try to sum up the last three chapters of **Mark**. Every serious inquirer should read at least this much of the New Testament for herself or himself. These chapters tell the story of the last days of Jesus on earth as a human being. To almost any inquirer, parts of these chapters will seem familiar, for they include the narrative of the last supper, which is acted out each week in some denominations in the commu nion service or in the Mass. Most denominations that do not hold a communion service each week do so once a month or at least four times a year. The Last Supper of Jesus and His disciples is described in Chapter 14. The three chapters, however, tell the entire story, that of Jesus' trial, crucifixion, death, resurrection, and final meetings with His followers. In slightly different ways, the other three gospels do the same, but Mark is supposed to have been written before the other three.

There are some who wish to follow the Christian way because they have tried other roads to happiness and have found them to be disappointing. Now they would like to try the Christian life. — I recommend it heartily, but not just because the Christian way incorporates a fine set of values. I recommend it because God showed us this way to the happy life, and I believe Him.

You may not be ready to decide that you can say yes to a belief in God, a belief in the Incarnation, and a belief in God's miracles. Not yet. But you would like to try the Christian way of life anyhow. In that case, I recall what the great London Methodist pastor Leslie Weatherhead said in his last book: He said he would ask any serious inquirer only to agree to follow Christ; then he would leave it up to the inquirer as to what specific details of belief should be added. — Why not? — But I personally find it easier to follow Christ because I believe in God and in the Incarnation.

CHAPTER TWELVE
Mainly About Paul
Selections from Acts: 1 and 2; 7:57- 8:3; 9:1-22; 17:18-34

Approximately one fourth of the New Testament was written by a man named Luke; his name is given to one of the four gospels, and he wrote the book entitled **The Acts of the Apostles**; we customarily refer to it simply as **Acts**. Much of that book tells of the missionary journeys of Paul, originally known by his Jewish name Saul. But the first two chapters are particularly important to Christians because they tell of what happened after the resurrection of Christ and through what we call Pentecost, when the apostles received the gift of the Holy Spirit (called Holy Ghost in earlier translations).

In **Acts 1:13** we have a list of the eleven apostles other than Judas Iscariot, the betrayer of Jesus. In 1:23-26, we have the story of the selection of Matthias to replace Judas and make the number of apostles again twelve.

In **Acts 2:1-6**, and after, we find the narrative of how the apostles received the Holy Spirit, which made it possible for them to go forth and preach the Christian message with divine inspiration.

In **Acts 7:57-8:3**, we encounter Paul (Saul) for the first time. That first encounter is strange indeed, however; for Saul is 'consenting unto' the death of the first Christian martyr, Stephen, who has just finished a sermon to the Jews around him before he is taken out and stoned.

Then, in chapter 9 of **Acts**, verses 1-22 (see also chapters 22 and 26, where Paul repeats the story), Luke tells us of Paul's dramatic conversion to Christianity, from having been a persecutor of all Christians to becoming one of the most industrious of Christian leaders. Because Paul was on the road to Damascus when he saw the light, we often refer to this as the Damascus Road Conversion. In summary, the voice of Jesus speaks to Paul and asks him why he is persecuting Christ and His church. Because of this experience, Paul makes his commitment to the cause of Christ. Eventually, Paul's missionary journeys, not only in the Middle East, but into what is now called Europe, are largely responsible for the growth of the Christian church; from the missionary Paul we can say our own opportunities for Christian service and knowledge came. The same Paul, we should remember, who had been a zealous persecutor of all Christians.

My personal selection of passages from **Acts** is not intended to limit your reading, either in this book or in the rest of the New Testament. The final selection I have included, one of many possibilities, is Paul's ser mon to the inquirers in Athens. It is often called the Mars' Hill sermon because it was there that he preached, at the re quest of the Athenian philosophers.

That sermon, I believe, is particularly appropriate for younger people of this time in history, our time; many are seeking here and there for some sort of guidance. They may dismiss Christianity because they have seen many members of Christian churches who have not lived as Christians according to New Testament standards. That, I believe, is like throwing out the baby with the bath water. We Christians are as murky and wrongheaded as we can be; but the Christian message — preserved, incidentally, by the very Christian churches which all of us must know are imperfect — is still there to light the serious inquirer's way to a happy life.

In view of the frequent falling away of Christians in an age of extended prosperity, either like our pre sent one or like some of the ages against which Amos and other Old Testament prophets preached, a serious inquirer today might well ask whether or not Christianity has ever worked. Such a question makes sense.

My answer is twofold: In the first place, in each of the dozen or so churches I have belonged to there have been some earnest Christians whose lives could hardly be criticized adversely by the most careful student of the New Testament and/or by the most severe critic of those brothers and sisters (imperfect like self) who go to church regularly. In every congregation there is a minority (sorry, but that must be the truth) of persons who hold up their own actions, rather than the actions of others, to the various tests of Christianity presented in the New Testament and do reasonably well in meeting them, recognizing in humility that they have sometimes missed the mark (an old definition of sin.) They have ex isted in every church I have belonged to, in five denomina tions and in five states. They often are not chosen for service on church boards; their genuine humility is sometimes at play here; but they are active, supporting members of their chur ches. Even if their total figures constitute no more than ten per cent of all church members (and I suspect that the percentage is higher than that), they make the churches worth saving, worth being a part of.

But, like many other Christians, I have seen whole groups of persons dominated by the Christian spirit working together cooperatively in a project that has proved that the Christian way of life really works, really brings hap piness to those who give it a fair trial in their lives. I have described one cooperative effort of just that sort in chapter 7.

From my personal observation of that one group of Christians, I take great solace and receive a renewal of faith whenever I begin to have doubts about the efficacy of the Christian prescription for happiness. It does work! I have seen it work with a large number of persons, as well as in isolated instances.

That was the Christian formula for happiness that Paul received and then transmitted to us today.

CHAPTER THIRTEEN
Flesh and Spirit
Galatians 5:19-26

Luke's gospel and Act's, also by Luke, make up about one fourth of the New Testament. The letters of Paul make up about another fourth.

One of the most famous passages in Paul's letters occurs in the little book of **Galatians**, chapter 5. It was probably one of the earliest portions of the New Testament written, and we should remember that it was a letter to a specific group of people, Christians who had stated off well on the Christian path, but then had taken one or more wrong turns. In this letter, Paul is scolding them and trying to point out, among other things, the way people outside the church act (according to the flesh, he says; we would call them 'streetwise') and how the Holy Spirit acting within us should make us act as Christians. The latter is one of the most treasured descriptions and prescriptions for the Christian life. The first is identifiable with what we see around us today, some of the paths non-Christians follow toward what they believe will be happiness.

How to Be Unhappy

Great theologians have determined precisely what Paul means by the word 'flesh' in this passage. I approximate its meaning by using the word **world**; in many cases, we can use that word so popular now **street-smart** or **street-wise**. I do not need to define it further, for to anyone who has been in college in the last ten or fifteen years, the meaning is clear. (I know that purists would use a hyphen, but I prefer to drop it most of the time and simply say **streetwise**.)

Now if you are looking for something better than the standard methods of becoming happy, you have probably already either tried or observed other people trying the items in Paul's list in verses 19-21. People who are streetsmart and go after the conventional goals of life today are likely to have been guilty of (without worrying about any such thing as guilt, of course) fornication, uncleanness, lasciviousness, and perhaps even adultery. After all, didn't Herbert Marcuse or his disciples say, 'If it feels good, do it!' and, just to make sure that the listeners could feel morally superior to others, 'Make love, not war'?

Also very frequently recommended by the streetsmart people were the use of drugs and drunkenness, and of course, revellings. Standard stuff, particularly on college campuses, where the streetwise often assembled.

Idolatry and witchcraft have also had their fans, even in the strict senses of the words. But more prevalent, I think, have been the creation of different types of idols than the old stone carvings once worshipped: photos of rock stars, film stars, and athletes; and for the older crowd, actual or remembered photos of 'the man of distinction,' the corporate CEO, and their like.

Witchcraft? You don't have to be a president's wife to follow horoscopes. And there is a good deal of ritual mumbo jumbo about most standard methods of having a good time, whether it involves just the right way to mix a Martini or the best shoes to wear for jogging. We do not use our minds to penetrate and discard the superfluous in life.

But what we really like to do is hate. We make ourselves miserable with it, and envying the success of other people, especially those not close to us — well, even those people — really uses up a lot of our energy. We make a political big deal out of everything that comes along (variance, partisanship), and we make even our games, intended for relaxation, opportunities for strife and wrath. — Sometimes our hatred even leads to murder; but if it does not, we seldom hesitate to kill our enemies off with gossip; by gossip, we can leave them walking around, apparently still alive, but dead as far as our little group is concerned.

Was Paul really writing to the people in galatia in the first century? He sounds as though he is writing to us today. I keep up with what is going on in our society by going to movies, watching television, and taking part in a few respectable nonchurch activities as well as in church, of course. There are all sorts of self-inflicted misery around me and in the society I see on film and read about in the other media. **Self-inflicted misery.** Paul described today very well.

How to be Happy

In **Galatians** 5:22-23, Paul gives us a description of the woman or man who is truly happy, a description of a Christian, one who has really taken to heart the lessons of Christ and who has abjured the teachings of the world outside the church. He tells us the qualities of character produced in those who have within them the Holy Spirit:

'But the fruit of the Spirit is love, joy, peace, long-suffering, gentleness, goodness, faith, meekness, temperance.'

What is the key to these two lists? To a large degree, it is in two words: selfishness and unselfishness. Most of the so-called 'wisdom' of those who claim to be streetsmart amounts really to being selfish, to putting oneself at the center of the universe. One who is guided by the Spirit, however, puts others before self; such a person is likely to be happy. Selfish, self-centered people — those I have known, at least — are seldom happy. And the kind of 'happiness' that self-centered persons claim to have, a happiness based on 'getting even' or getting ahead of others, is usually self-destructive. In seventy-one years, I have never known a single person who was full of hate and jealousy and vengefulness who was really happy. For those I have known well, I have felt sorry. How much they have missed in life!

As to the list itself, little needs to be said. I would like to point out one word, however, the second in the list is **joy**. Often being a Christian is considered to be a gloomy, dour, solemn matter. Not so! A Christian is considerate of others, it is true; hence there can be no jesting at the expense of others. But that is, after all, a poor way to seek for joy. There is great joy in doing good, in performing Christ's services to shut-ins and the sick, for example. And in such visits, one can often turn sadness into cheer by good conversation, particularly with someone seriously ill or dying, someone condemned not only to pain and suffering, but to sorrow and gloom as well.

Each of the qualities in Paul's list is deserving of analysis, reflection, and appreciation. It is a great list. I know one youngish Methodist minister who has a vanity license plate (given him by a relative) on his car that sums up these qualities, qualities which he has, which Catholic priests I have known had, and which Christians of various denominations have.

We should not expect to acquire these qualities without trouble, of course. We have to work at them, regularly, never assuming that we have them forever. Being a Christian really does take work; one can never, never become complacent; that way lies pride, a feeling of moral superiority, and, of course, the negation of consideration for all other human beings. Becoming complacent about oneself is a sure way to lose the good things that God has provided; it is a form of substituting self for God.

Paul knew how difficult it was to be a Christian, how easy it was to make mistakes. In **Romans**, a letter sometimes called Paul's systematic exposition of his theology — his interpretation of the total meaning of God and of Christ — Paul tells us how hard it is, at times, to be a Christian:

'For I know that in me (that is, in my flesh,) dwelleth no good thing: for to will is present with me; but how to perform that which is good I find not.

For the good that I would I do not: but the evil which I would not, that I do.'

It may be little comfort for any of us when we have failed to know that Paul confessed failure, too. But I personally find that I feel a little less guilty than I otherwise would when I know that Paul also tried and sometimes failed. Paul offers a theological explanation of this failure which you may read for yourself. One of the passages in **Romans** in which I find great comfort is Paul's reminder that we always have Christ's love, even in our mistakes: 'Who shall separate us from the love of Christ? Shall tribulation, or distress, or persecution, or famine, or nakedness, or peril, or sword?' (**Romans 8:35**.) His answer (verse 37) is: 'Nay, in all these things we are more than conquerors through him who loved us.' I do not stop reading at this point, nor should you.

For me, it has also been a great source of comfort to have read a little book by John R. W. Stott, **Baptism and Fullness**, A very holy man and a gifted interpreter of scripture, Stott explains how, even though we have been granted the gift of the Holy Spirit to guide us, we sometimes do un christian things. — When I say that this little book has been a com fort to me, I should add that it is also a warning to me not to imagine that whatever I do as a follower of Christ is sure to be what Christ would have done. — That would be substituting myself for God.

If we pledge ourselves to follow Christ, we will not always do the right thing. But over the long years of trying to be Christians, we shall have the chance to develop those qualities Paul says are produced by the Holy Spirit. We shall have a vision of what it is to be happy, and, at least much of the time, we can experience that happiness.

CHAPTER FOURTEEN:
Christian Love
I Corinthians 13

The word in the Greek is **agape**. We know that it means something different from eros, the love bet ween the sexes, and phileo, love for a brother or sister. Agape is unselfish, unconditional, fully-committed love for whatever its object is, a person, a Being, or an idea. So when we read I **Corinthians 13**, Paul's great and poetic essay on Christian love, we should not confuse it with anything less than what I have described. Most contemporary translations of the Bible that I have used translate the word **agape** as simply **love**. Fine! So long as we do not confuse it with sexual passion, which usually includes a certain amount of lust, or self-centered desire, no matter what other qualities may be involved. — Nor do we wish to confuse it with friendship, such as the close friendship between siblings. It is more than that.

The King James translation of the Bible, completed in 1611, while Shakespeare was still alive and using the language of that day, is beautiful. From that version the quotations I have used so far have come. (It is also long out of copyright, another reason for me to use it.) But the King James translation uses the word **charity** to translate **agape**, and the word charity today connotes a certain amount of condescension toward the object; one unfortunately feels superior to the person to whom one shows charity. Modern translations use the English word love, as I have said, but so does at least one popular English translation earlier than the King James version, the famous Geneva Bible of 1560, supposedly us ed by Shakespeare. Modernizing the spellings a bit, I present the translation of I **Corinthians 13** from that version:

'Though I speak with the tongues of men and angels, and have not love, I am as sounding brass, or a tinkling cymbal.

And though I have the gift of prophecy, and knew all secrets and all knowledge, yea, if I had all faith, so that I could remove mountains and had not love, I were nothing.

And though I feed the poor with all my goods, and though I give my body, that I be burned, and have not love, it profiteth me nothing.

Love suffreth long: it is beautiful: love envieth not; love doth not boast itself: it is not puffed up.

It disdaineth not: it seeketh not her own things: it is not provoked to anger: it thinketh not evil:

It rejoiceth not in iniquity, but rejoiceth in the truth:

It suffreth all things: it believeth all things: it hopeth all things: it endureth all things:

Love doth never fall away, though that prophesying be abolished, or the tongues cease, or knowledge vanish away.

For we know in part, and we prophesy in part.

But when that which is perfect is come, then that which is in part shall be abolished.

When I was a child, I spake as a child, I understood as a child, I thought as a child: but when I became a man, I put away childish things.

For now we see through a glass darkly: but then shall we see face to face. Now I know in part: but then shall I know even as I am known.

And now abideth faith, hope, and love, even these three: but the chiefest of these is love.'

— It is a good idea to have seen at least one earlier translation than the King James version; great as that translation was, we can see that it owed much to what had gone before.

St. Augustine is said to have called Christianity the religion of love. Unlike the followers of other religions, then, we do not have the right to hate. Unless we can love our enemies, even, as Christ tells us, we have missed the mark in our religion. No matter what we do, how wise we are, how much we are willing to sacrifice, unless we can have and show our love for others, we are nothing.

This passage goes against just about everything the streetsmarts advise. Having seen the results of being streetsmart, I can only say that Paul is correct in what he says. There has to be something better than selfishness. Paul says there is. It is love. That is Christianity.

In our focus on the central theme of this passage, we often miss some of the incidental points made in these verses. One of the most important, in my opinion, is Paul's recognition that now, in this life, with imperfect human minds, we can only know in part. God's mind is perfect; our minds are not. When we hate, and when we go on violent crusades against other people, often we do so because we believe we know all that God knows. The Canadian theologian Charles Davis calls our 'lust for certitude' one of the greatest temptations of our religion. He says it is important to search for meaning; it may be dangerous to insist that we have found it. Someone else, Gide, I believe, advises: 'Follow those who seek the truth. Beware of those who have found it.' Perhaps, thinking of what Paul says in this great passage, we might be particularly aware of the danger of thinking we have found what is in God's mind. If we believe that we have the truth, and that no one else has it, we are likely to fall into the trap of hating anyone who disagrees with our own conclusions. Our conclusions, the theologian Karl Barth suggests, should be held humbly, with the full knowledge that we could be wrong. We must have our own conclusions, of course, subject to change as we make new discoveries, but it is most dangerous to say that they are God's truths.

I **Corinthians 13** deserves rereading frequently.

CHAPTER FIFTEEN:
How Christians Should Live
Romans 12

Experts say that Paul often discusses the theory of the Christian message in the first part of his letters, then, in the final portion, tells his readers what they should do, how they should apply the theory to their daily lives. Chapter 12 of the book of Romans does just that.

First, he advises Christians to make the right kind of sacrifice, not a burnt offering, not a few coins or even a tithe, but a full commitment to Christ: 'Present your body as a living sacrifice.' (Body refers to the complete person, physical as well as intellectual and spiritual.) A full commitment to Christ! — How logical! Yet how often ignored in favor of a part-time commitment of life and money. Persons outside the church have often ridiculed the inconsistency of those who go to church on Sunday, support the church with a portion of their funds and even with a few hours of their time now and then, but otherwise follow the advice of the streetsmarts, excusing themselves by saying that, 'Everybody does it. If you want to survive in this world, you gotta go with the flow. — Do what everyone else does.'

Not so, Paul tells us. We are to make a full commitment to Christ, and we are not to be 'conformed to this world.' Instead, we should make those changes in our lives that enable us to conform to the will of God.

It is strange to think about, but I have sometimes heard intelligent people outside the church object that they could never accept the restrictions imposed on them by following the Ten Commandments , one clear expression of the will of God; yet those same intelligent people conform to whatever their peers may tell them is the way to get ahead in this world. They choose to be streetsmart, of course, but certainly not Christian! Like most of us, intelligent or otherwise, they do not see the inconsistency in their behavior.

Paul says we must not be conformed to this world, but be 'transformed.' Becoming a Christian requires the determination to make just such a complete change in one's life. As Christ tells us, we cannot serve both God and Mammon (which stands for the worship of money.)

Paul goes on: Knowing how prone we are to becoming proud, particularly when our lives suggest that we are morally superior to our neighbors, Paul cautions each of us 'not to think of himself more highly than he ought to think.' We are to retain a balance in our thoughts, one that enables us to 'think soberly, according as God hath dealt to every man the measure of faith.'

Then Paul tells us to use our gifts from God, our special talents, cooperatively and wisely. He does not tell us to hire a professional Christian and leave all of the work of Christian service to that person; instead, he breaks down the work too often assigned to one professional pastor into: preaching, serving others (ministering), exhorting, ruling, showing mercy, and so forth. — This is what is meant by full commitment to Christ: serving Him in whatever capacity our talents make it possible for us to serve.

But Paul says it better than I could, I think. Here is the rest of the chapter, according to the translators brought together by King James:

'Let love be without dissimulation. Abhor that which is evil; cleave to that which is good.

Be kindly affectioned one to another with brotherly love; in honour preferring one another;

Not slothful in business; fervent in spirit; serving the Lord;

Rejoicing in hope; patient in tribulation; continuing instance in prayer;

Distribute to the necessity of saints; given to hospitality.

Bless those which persecute you: bless, and curse not.

Rejoice with them that do rejoice, and weep with them that weep.

Be of the same mind one toward another. Mind not high things, but condescend to men of low estate. Be not wise in your own conceits .

Recompense to no man evil for evil. Provide things honest in the sight of all men.

If it be possible, as much as lieth in you, live peaceably with all men.

Dearly beloved, avenge not yourselves, but rather give place unto wrath: for it is written, Vengeance is mine; I will repay, saith the Lord.

Therefore if thine enemy hunger, feed him; if he thirst, give him drink: for in so doing thou shalt heap coals of fire on his head.

Be not overcome of evil, but overcome evil with good.'

I have heard two quite different speculations about the meaning of heaping 'coals of fire'one the head of an enemy one has helped. Both make sense. I do not think anyone will have much trouble in understanding it today, however; for the streetsmart say, 'Don't get mad; get even.' We know quite well how the selfish person's mind works, and we can guess that some intelligent but self-centered persons might be so surprised at seeing Christians return evil with good that they would be hot with embarrassment and with humiliation at how base they themselves have been.

But don't count on it. Our society has been brainwashed into self-centeredness for a long time. Some of its citizens are dead and would need more than a kind deed to be recalled to life.

Christians do good instead of evil because that way brings happiness, and it is the will of God.

PART TWO
A GUIDE TO VISITING CHURCHES

CHAPTER ONE
WHY PEOPLE GO TO CHURCH

If you go to church because you know that you have been a sinner and you need help in making more sense out of life than you have made so far, you have the best possible attitude for becoming a good disciple of Christ. In Luke 18, Jesus tells a parable that will be useful to keep in mind as we think of the people we shall meet when we go to church:

'Two men went up into the temple to pray; the one a Pharisee, the other a publican.

The Pharisee stood and prayed thus with himself, God, I thank thee, that I am not as other men are, extortioners, unjust, adulterers, or even as this publican.

I fast twice in the week, I give tithes of all that I possess.

And the publican, standing afar off, would not lift up so much as his eyes unto heaven, but smote upon his breast, saying, God be merciful to me a sinner.

I tell you, this man went down to his house justified rather than the other; for every one that exalteth himself shll be abased; and he that humbleth himself shall be exalted.'

— We have that parable before us when we go to church, a parable taught by Jesus, the Christ who was crucified by the religious leaders of His time, including the Pharisees. And yet we often exhibit that moral superiority which all readers must find to be so ridiculous in the Pharisse of this parable. Remember the Elder Brother in the parable of the Prodigal Son? Jesus was teaching the same lesson there, too, wasn't He? And remember the narrative about that good Jewish prophet Jonah? Jonah was also reluctant to see God's mercy for sinners.

We haven't changed since those days; not all of us, at least. I remember with shame, but very distinctly, an occasion when a well-dressed man came into church a bit late and sat on my left (my family, on the right, had to scoot down the pew a bit): the man smelled heavily of whiskey or of some other hard liquor and had evidently come into the service after a Saturday night of drinking. At the time, I shrank from his touch, almost by instinct. Perhaps I felt insecure about my own temptations to sin and did not wish to be identified with him; I do not know the explanation. But I do know that I wanted to establish my moral superiority to the man, perhaps a penitent wishing to give Christianity a chance. I did not help matters much. In the same circumstances, other regular church members, even though they know better, may not help mat ters much in your case.

I ask only that you give us more than one chance, and do not judge us too harshly. We are sinners like you. Sometimes we forget, as did the Pharisee in the parable Jesus tells us.

There are good reasons for going to church, however. In many, perhaps most, churches, you will be worshipping alongside other repentant sinners who, like yourself want to make sense out of this life they have been given. Perhaps they have tried other ways and have not felt that either wealth or power or status or pleasure or self-development kept its promise of happiness for the worshipper. Now they, like you, want to try Christianity. Well, the institutional church is about the only place they can find it. Although that church has many faults, there are no other real competitors , not in the task of providing Christian meaning for life.

In fact, one of the problems with the institutional church is that often it tries to compete with other groups in the community in what they do, thereby neglecting its own exclusive mission: to provide Christian meaning for human life. In part because the church tries to do other kinds of work, however, you will find many church members who are primarily in church for some other reason than the one you are there for.

The Mammonists

It is absolutely true that some people join churches because they believe it is good for business. I use the word **join** deliberately, for such persons often develop other reasons for belonging to the churches they join; the business uses of membership may actually become unimportant over time. A number of those I have associated with have become exceptionally good Christians, for one reason or another, and the reason why they originally joined the church becomes no reason at all for continuing to belong.

Ironically, most of us like to be able to trust the persons we do business with, and when a bank vice president, say, becomes a conscientious Christian after join ing a church primarily to develop business contacts, that banker may find that his or her associates in the church, because they have learned to trust the banker, are more likely to do business with that person than they were when the banker was most interested in the church as a source of business contacts. — Does that make sense? It does to me, and my comment comes from having known several bank executives who were also church leaders.

To the critic outside the church, however, the banker or investment counselor or insurance salesperson or store manager who belongs to a church congregation seems to be using the church for selfish reasons. I have known only a few, a very few, who have done this; but any person in business is more likely to be slandered in such matters than, say, a teacher like me.

Are there any who worship Mammon? Yes. Are there any who once worshipped Mammon exclusively, but now have made a full commitment to Christ? Yes, again. Almost all of those who continue to worship Mammon only have remain ed outside the church. It is easier that way.

The Reformers: Social and Political

I have taken part in social and political reform groups in my community and in national movements. But **using** a church has always seemed to me to be a waste of time. Why not take the direct route and work within a political party or within a group dedicated to promoting one specific cause? Church is something else, I have felt. You do not **use** God to promote your own political and social programs.

Yet I may be wrong. In the 1988 campaign for the Presidency, for example, one candidate in each party permitted the continued use of the title Reverend. To me, that seemed to be **using** God for one's own purposes. So many members of Roman Catholic orders got into politics in the United States that the Pope issued an order which, as I, an outsider, understood it, gave those who had taken religious vows a choice: either leave the order and run for or accept office or get out of politics and keep your original vows. — No doubt I am oversimplifying that order. Professional clergy often have the temptation to go into politics. If they do, unfortunately, no one else will do their work for them; if they do not, someone **else** will work at political and social reform.

But we assume that the professional clergy, by and large, believe in God and have as their first goal in life making this a more Christian world. We cannot always make such an assumption about ordinary church members. From my own profession, teaching, come many who feel that belonging to a local church is a good idea, but more because the church stands for and does good in the world than because they believe in God. To them it seems quite logical that they should be active in their churches, win election to office in the local and regional and national governing bodies of the denomination, and support resolutions that they consider to be good for the country, for humanity in general. — I have known both college and high school teachers of this nature. Not many of them have studied the Christian religion past the age of fourteen, but they have, in many cases, sat at the feet of college professors of sociology, political science, economics, psychology, and the like. With such an imbalance of knowledge, it is natural that many would be dedicated to the causes of social and political reform, as their professors have defined reform.

Do such persons exist in the churches? Certainly. Are their motives always clear? No. Not even to themselves. It is easy to confuse the many ideas one has heard in a college class in sociology with the paltry few one has encountered in junior high Sunday School or confirmation classes. Who can really blame them?

But they may sometimes make the Christian religion sound very much like what you have heard Dr. _____ say in a college class in one of the social sciences. The Christian religion is not the same, not at all. Please do not permit yourself to be confused.

Other Types of Church Members

There are, of course, some people in the church who are not at all sure that there is a God, but who give token support to some church because they wish to pur chase what is often called 'fire insurance.' You may meet such persons in a church, but not too often, for they are more likely to appear at an ice cream social or a church supper than at a service of worship. — This statement is not intended to be sarcastic; it comes from my experiences as a pastor, where often I met absolute strangers at social events, people who claimed to be on the church rolls, but who were seldom if ever in church on Sundays.

There are probably quite a few members of church congregations who have joined because the church seems a better place than a tavern to meet other people and socialize with them. They may also find a church a good place to bring up children, with not only pleasant Sunday School classes to attend, but also a variety of youth activities of a wholesome nature. Few churches are so intrusive in other aspects of one's social life that they interfere with one's joining another kind of social club, either.

How many church members would be left if we dropped all of those who joined the churches for reasons other than making a serious commitment to Christ? I do not know. In some churches, however, you should expect to find only a minority who firmly believe in the existence of God and who have made a serious commitment to serving Christ. — Perhaps in God's mind, even a small minority may be significant, however. We can see such forces at work in some aspects of nature: the spreading of seeds, for example. Who can Say?

In Defense of Churches

Remember the parable of the Pharisee and the Publican? That parable applies to all of us. First, it applies to me, for I really cannot judge other people I meet in church, even after talking with them over the years, working with them on committees and boards, even serving them as their pastor. Second, it applies to you, the reader, the person outside the church, sitting in judgment on the church. As I believe is the case, at least, only God can truly see into the hearts of other human beings. Sometimes I have found them to be better than I had thought them to be; and that may be a judgment against me, not against them.

Then there is always the possibility of change for the better if one belongs to a church and takes a regular part in it. In my own life, I have found that the slow and agonizing death of a loved one has made the church more real to me, its value clearer. Other people, I have been told often, have gone through the same kind of experience, the same kind of enlightenment. And that can happen to anyone who maintains a regular relationship with a Christian church: someone in business, someone who has a college major in the social sciences, someone who has joined the church primarily because it is a good social club, or even someone who has maintained a loose sort of relationship with a church for what is considered to be its fire insurance value. I have known people in all of these categories who have had life experiences that have made them better Christians than they were before.

Good Christians? Who can say? I cannot claim to be a good Christian now, though I am trying; but I do believe that I understand Christianity better now than I did before my first wife died. The church means a great deal to me.

Christianity means unselfishness and service to others, love for others, even enemies. I know this. But I also know that most of us originally join a church for selfish reasons. Some of us, like me and perhaps like you, join it in order to obtain meaning for life, Christian meaning. We want to make some kind of sense out of life while we are living, and we hope that we can find it in the Christian churches.

I believe we can. But I do believe, as well, that a serious inquirer needs a few warnings about what may lie ahead. In my opinion, Christian meaning for life can be found in either the Roman Catholic, the Mainline Protestant, or the Conservative Protestant churches. But the inquirer may be easily turned off by a single encounter, too. My intent in the future chapters of this book is to help you avoid stumbling in your search for Christian meaning.

CHAPTER TWO
THREE WAYS TO CHRISTIAN LIVES

Between July of 1991 and July of 1993, Mrs. Otto and I visited one hundred churches in thirty-three denominations. This was part of our research for writing this book. We learned that we could be comfortable in all of those churches, at least by the second or third visit to a church of a particular denomination. Not everyone could adjust so readily to so many different kinds of churches, I suppose, but the experience demonstrated to me that any initial discomfort is likely to disappear within a short time. The same can be said of a strange church in a denomination similar to one that is familiar.

Let me illustrate: Mrs. Otto had been a Lutheran for more than fifty years when we married (both of us having been widowed), but after a few visits to the large Presbyterian church where I lived, she chose to become a Presbyterian; I had already volunteered to become a Lutheran if she wished to remain in that denomination for my past experience in churches had taught me that the particular denomination one belongs to is only one of the factors to consider in choosing a church, and not always the most important one.

Nevertheless, habit and comfort can be important to most people. Other factors being equal, one should consider going back to the kind of church in which one grew up. Even a single bad experience in a particular church may not be a good reason for leaving one denomination and going to another. The serious inquirer may find Christian meaning for life in either the Roman Catholic Church, the Mainline Protestant Church, or the Conservative Protestant Church. I could comfortably be a member of any of the thirty-three denominations we visited, but if I were to move to another town, I should probably join a church in a denomination I am accustomed to.

When one truly decides to take seriously his or her association with a church, however, it is not a bad idea to look around for a time, perhaps for from three to six months. I do not recommend more than six months, for it is all too easy to put off making any decision at all, then to quit looking. There will be no perfect church; as my father once said to a critic of his church, if the critic decided to join, it would immediately become imperfect, whatever it was before. — The point is: Don't look for the perfect church; but do join a church.

The three major kinds of Christian church have a number of important differences. There are exterior differences, of course, but they also differ in other ways, sometimes in ways that are hard to define. Let us take these differences one at a time.

Exterior Differences

When I was a boy, there seemed to be a different kind of church architecture for Catholic and Protestant churches, at least in my home town. If a church had a cross on it, it was probably Catholic. At least, that is my memory of the times. Although I have seen some local church buildings designed to fit a specific denomination's order of worship, such cases are rare. For example, one synagogue of the reformed Jewish faith in Des Moines was, we were told, designed by an architect who was a Presbyterian. The current rabbi of that synagogue told us that the Presbyterian's ideas of Jewish symbolism were rather eccentric. I have seen the same eccentricity in Protestant church designs and decorations. (The painting behind a baptistry in one church that believed only in adult baptism by immersion had to be replaced because the artist had illustrated the use of sprinkling for baptism.)

The exterior architecture of a church building today seldom reveals its denomination, however. One Catholic priest told our class of visiting a worship service in an Episcopal church that was almost impossible to distinguish from a Roman Catholic service; the building itself was, if anything, more Catholic than that of a Catholic church. I personally know of Methodist and Lutheran church buildings that are no different on the outside than Roman Catholic churches were in my youth. I also know of Roman Catholic church buildings erected since 1960 that are no different from a large church intended for use by a Presbyterian, U.C.C., Baptist, or Methodist institution.

Inside the church building, however, there is a difference, with only a few exceptions that I have seen.

Normally, the interior of a Roman Catholic church building is quite ornate, with religious scenes on the windows, the walls, the dome (if the church has one), and behind the rail that usually separates the altar and pulpit area from the people in the pews. (Catholics refer to this area behind the rail as the sanctuary, whereas Protestants sometimes use that term to apply to the entire auditorium of worshippers.) In each pew in a Roman Catholic church, there is usually a padded kneeling bench that folds out from behind the seat ahead of one; there are times in the service when the worshipper stands, other times for sitting, and still other times for kneeling. There is definitely an altar in a Roman Catholic sanctuary; because the mass is a service of communion, a reenactment of the Last Supper, that altar is associated with the bread and wine, the elements of that sacrificial meal.

The interiors of Protestant churches tend to be less ornate, though many of them include stained glass windows. An occasional large illustration of a religious scene may also appear, sometimes over the baptistry, sometimes behind the altar, usually smaller than those found in Catholic churches, sometimes centrally located behind the pulpit or choir area. But there still remains some distinction between the decorated interiors of a Catholic and a Protestant church.

We should add that in many Protestant churches there is no altar at all. Some of these churches, however, give prominence to the communion table. In some Protestant churches, the pulpit is still centrally located, for the sermon was for decades the focus of the Protestant worship service.

But the dominant feature of the traditional Protestant church was its plainness, inside and out. There are still remnants of this influence in Protestant churches, just as most older Roman Catholic churches retain a good deal of ornateness. But what we call the spirit of ecumenism has helped bring about the disappearance of such traditional marks of one basic branch of Christianity or another.

Worship

Whatever I say about differences in churches must be in the form of generalities, and as you must have heard from some teacher somewhere, 'all generalities are false, including this one.' I am very much aware of the danger of forming and using stereotypes of either individuals or groups. Someone has said that only bigots and scholars apply stereotypes to people. Please remember that caution as you read on.

To an outsider like me, at least, Catholics seem to be able to separate fellowship from worship more clearly than Protestants do. This may be, in part at least, because there is likely to be a completely separate fellowship hall, separate from the church building, and entered by members of the parish in an entirely different mood than many Protestants have when they enter their church buildings.

Protestants sometimes refer to a fellowship hall, but usually it is in the same building as what we Protestants usually call the sanctuary, the place for worship. The Protestant fellowship hall may even be used for some worship services or for a part of the Sunday School program. Protestant churches often make a big point of meeting friends and other members of the congregation over coffee before or after a worship service, too. Either fellowship is a more important part of a Protestant church than of a Catholic church or the activities of worship and fellowship are so completely separated in Catholic churches that the outsider cannot quite grasp the significance of fellowship activities to Catholics. In any case, Catholics separate the two sharply.

As a consequence, the Protestant who visits a Catholic church may feel, during much of the time at least, that individual church members are isolated from others. The person with a Catholic background who visits a Protestant church, on the other hand, may be shocked at the casual movement of one individual or a group from one part of the worship area to another, shaking hands, smiling, chatting, even calling across two or three rows of pews to friends they see. Often this kind of noisy exchange is discouraged by pastor and church board members, but it seems to be a part of the tradition in many Protestant churches. The separateness of some Protestant communities in the distant past, the use of the local Protestant church as a community center on the American frontier, or simply the difference in size between the average Protestant church (about 250 members) and the average Catholic parish (several times that figure, in the United States, at least) may have had more influence on these two distinct traditions than the religions have had. The differences seem to exist.

Before the collective service of worship begins, Protestants sometimes seem to be noisy. Catholics, on the other hand, genuflect (half-kneel) as they enter a pew, pull down the kneeling bench, and kneel in prayer for some time before they sit down and wait for the service to begin. They do this in quiet; only once in our many visits to Catholic churches have we heard anyone talking aloud, and in that case, from what was said, I gathered that the talker was an older woman who was not Catholic, probably on a visit to a son or daughter who had married into the Catholic Church.

Perhaps I should add that outside the worship area there is usually a font for holy water, which many Catholics dip their fingers in before entering the worship area. In my own visits, I have never done so, for it would have no real significance for me, a visitor. Neither have I taken communion in a Catholic church, though I have in the other denominations we have visited whenever communion was a part of the service. I do not wish to give offense to any Christian.

Once the prelude on the organ or piano begins, most Protestants quiet down and pay attention to the service in which they will take part. Typically, except in Episcopal and some Lutheran churches, a Protestant church provides a bulletin to each worshipper, one that lists the order of worship, the hymns and the page on which each is to be found in the hymnal, and some liturgical elements which the pastor and the worship committee of the church have decided to incorporate into the service: prayers of confession, other kinds of prayers, litanies of dedication and consecration, and the like. As I write this, an expanded use of liturgy is occurring in the Protestant fold in general, particularly in the so-called Mainline Protestant denominations. Various in fluences have brought about this trend, and by the time you read this, the fad may be over, but just now it exists.

The order of worship is not fixed, but a sort of standard pattern has existed in many Protestant denominations for some decades. Adapted from what is called the 'brief form' of the order of worship presented in a United Methodist hymnal of the 1960's is the following:

* Prelude
* Call to Worship
* Hymn (The people standing)
* Invocation (A prayer to God to become a partof the service, with sometimes a prayer of confession and the Lord's Prayer.)
* Responsive Reading (Hymnal or bulletin)
* Anthem (Usually the choir or a soloist)
* The Scripture Lessons Affirmation of Faith (People standing, creed, etc.)
* Pastoral Prayer
* Offertory and Announcements
* Hymn (The people standing)
* The Sermon Invitation to Christian Discipleship
* Hymn (The people standing)
* Benediction
* Postlude

Any Protestant will be sure to see that many departures from the order of worship above may be found in almost any local church. Nevertheless, it is a good standard to refer to if you have not been in the churchgoing habit for a few years or, if you have been raised in a Catholic or orthodox tradition. What are often referred to as Pentecostal churches or charismatic churches such as the Assembly of God churches, usually have several 'choruses' projected on a white wall at the front of the church or on a movie screen in that vicinity. In those churches, the people in attendance may stand for as much as twenty minutes or more, singing over and over the various choruses, usually led by an assistant in charge of singing. When the worshippers at last sit down, they may have the feeling of having participated very fully in the service; just physical weariness can help produce such a feeling. Because of the popularity of such choruses in charismatic services, I assume, some other Conservative Protestant churches use them, as well, although participants usually do not stand for such a length of time as in the charismatic churches.

As a matter of honesty, I should add that, as an English teacher, I do not like the seemingly monotonous repetition of trite phrases one finds in these choruses. They do, however, seem to belong to the same tradition as the famous and very popular 'Blowing in the Wind,' which Bob Dylan made famous around 1968. At that time, a teacher of religion at a Presbyterian college, a man ten years older than I was, even, complained to his students about the almost complete absence of theological content in Dylan's song and in others like it. He was probably right, and yet I think that he missed the point; so do I when I attend such a service. The repeated words and rhythm have, I am sure, a liturgical effect — that is, the same effect that liturgies have traditionally had in religious worship. That effect is nonverbal, but real.

With such an overview, you should be able to visit most Protestant churches without many surprises. It is useful to remember that, as Dr. George Forell has pointed out, in America we borrow from our competitors. He says that in this country Protestant churches not only borrow from one another whatever seems to be attractive to prospective Christians, but also borrow from Catholic churches, one of the reasons I am sure, that liturgy is very popular just now. Protestants have borrowed the idea.

What are the liturgical churches?

Those we generally refer to by this name are the Roman Catholic Church, the Eastern (Greek, Russian, etc.) Orthodox Churches, the Episcopal (Anglican) Church, and the Lutheran churches. Because a detailed explanation of the liturgy of each of these churches would take up many pages in this book and because learning to understand the liturgy will be one of your principal studies in preparation for membership in any of these churches, I shall not even attempt to explain them in detail at this point — and I am sure that any explanation I might attempt would be full of inaccuracies, in any case. What I can do, I hope, is to prepare you to visit one of these fine churches with some advance understanding of what to expect. Not enough, perhaps, but enough, I believe, to help you appreciate something of the values of a liturgical form of worship.

All of these churches follow a formal ritual in their worship service. Each prayer, response, proclamation, and inspirational reading is established not for a single local church, but for churches of that denomination everywhere for that particular Sunday or other worship day. The rituals vary somewhat from one season of the church year to another and from one Sunday to another, but the ritual is the same everywhere in the denomination that day. This sameness applies to the readings from scripture, which are established in all churches by a lectionary. (Many Mainline Protestant pastors follow a lectionary of readings from scripture, as well, a practice that has grown in the 1980's and 1990's.) The result, then, except for the sermon, is likely to be a worship service that is approximately the same wherever a particular language is used. — Prior to the second Vatican council, which changed the Roman Catholic Church in many ways, Latin was used throughout the world for church services; at that time, a worship service in a Roman Catholic Church in London or New York was almost exactly the same as one in Berlin or Rome or Mexico City. Since Vatican II, however, the vernacular (the language of the country) has been authorized and used in Roman Catholic churches; even so, the worship service is approximately the same except for the language it is in.

Such a ritualized service is, in effect, a great church drama. In recent times, at least, the nonclergy in the Catholic Church have been widely encouraged to read parts assigned to them in their missals and thus be an active part of the worship service; at other times, of course, they are encouraged to participate by listening and observing the rest of the drama.

In a Lutheran church, the person attending the worship service will find a hymnal in the pew rack which has in it not only hymns to be used in the service, but also the various parts of the worship service ritual. Usually a church bulletin will indicate the pages on which the various parts of the worship ritual are to be found, and the hymns will be listed either in the bulletin or on a board at the front of the room. Mrs. Otto, having been a Lutheran for more than fifty years, has no difficulty in following the service in that church, of course, but I have had to fumble somewhat, glancing at her hymnal page from time to time to follow the service accurately. On two formal visits to Lutheran churches, I found it very, very easy to take part in the service; one was part of the Evangelical Lutheran Church (relatively liberal, more or less like Mainline Protestant churches); the other was a Missouri Synod Lutheran Church (one of the two or three denominations of Lutheranism that are quite conservative): in each case, the large church printed the complete service, with all responses, in the bulletin. Those services were no more difficult for me, with my nonliturgical past, than were the services of other Protestant churches.

In an Episcopal church, one will also find in the pew racks the necessary materials for taking part in the worship service; in this case, a separate Book of Common Prayer, where one may find the readings for the day. A church bulletin usually provides help, and whenever you are in doubt, you may glance at a neighbor's page, as I did in the Lutheran churches we visited (the neighbor being my ex-Lutheran wife) or, if necessary, simply look puzzled and silently seek help from a neighbor. I have always been able to get by in this way.

We did attend one Greek Orthodox church in nearby Decatur, Illinois; there the people were exceptionally friendly and helpful, and we were provided with Greek-English versions of the worship service. We derived great delight, however, from simply watching and listening. The priest, relatively new to America, was inspiring in his role, and the singers made the strange words sound beautiful and full of praise. It was a fine experience; and we are sure that if we had continued to go there, we would have found it a good place to worship God; God is the same, we have found, no matter where He is worshipped.

As I am sure you know, the Greek (and other Eastern) Orthodox Church was a sibling church to the Roman Catholic Church; both of them have elements in their services going back to ancient Jewish times, as do the Episcopal and Lutheran churches. Episcopalians are a part of the international group of churches stemming from the Church Of England. The first pastors in the Church of England had previously been priests in the Roman Catholic Church. Martin Luther, too, as you probably know, was a Roman Catholic priest and theology teacher when he began the steps toward founding the Lutheran Church. It is easy to see, then, why all of these churches are what is called liturgical churches.

The Wesley brothers, who founded the Methodist Church, were originally members of the Church Of England. If you turn back to the brief order of worship on an earlier page, you will see many of the elements of almost any liturgical service: a call to worship, an invocation, prayers of confession, prayers of praise and thanksgiving, scripture readings, a sermon, a benediction, psalms and hymns of praise, and so forth. These elements are usually in liturgies of worship, too, and the influence of the Roman Catholic Church may be found in Episcopal, Lutheran, Methodist, and other churches, as well. You may wish to think about the elements of Christian worship and sort them out as you visit churches. Hymns and choruses incorporate one or more of these elements, and one can say that all churches are liturgical, a few more than the others.

Until now, we have said nothing really about the service of communion, the Lord's Supper, the Eucharist, as it is variously termed. We have said that it is observed each week or oftener in some denominations, once a month in some, once each quarter in others. In the Roman Catholic Church, the service of communion is the Mass. Every Sunday and most other days of the week during the year that service is the climax of the worship service in a Catholic Church. That service is typically divided into two parts: a service of preparation and the Eucharist.

At first, the members of the church in the pews, the priest(s) celebrating the worship of God enter in processional, advance to the altar area, kiss the altar in reverence, and thereafter lead the service of worship. Appropriate hymns and readings and prayers occur during the service that follows. There will be three readings from the scriptures: one from the Old Testament, one from the Epistles or Acts or Revelation, and one from a Gospel. All persons present will, as designated, sound out praise after the Gospel reading. Then the priest will give a homily (sermon, though shorter in most cases than a typical Protestant sermon). This is followed by a gerneral profession of faith in the form of a creed, then intercessory prayers.

After this introductory phase, the celebration of the Eucharist begins. The altar is prepared, a Eucharistic prayer is given by the priest, the Lord's Prayer and the sign of peace are given by the people, the priest prepares the elements of the Supper, the bread and the wine, and they are distributed to the members of the congregation who wish to receive them (coming to the front of the church as called). After communion is over, the priest prepares the members of the church to go forth into the world and be the ministers (servants) of Christ. Then the priest blesses the other worshippers (gives a benediction).

Now, how does a visitor to a Roman Catholic church find out what he or she is to do in the service? Usually there is a missal for the season (a little paperback book) which has in it special prayers and responses for the particular day. Catholic churches are often quite large, and as a consequence, the visitor may feel that it is more difficult to obtain help from others in the pews, but I have received such help. Finding a missal takes time, so I advise a visitor to get there early; look at the back of the church for a stack of missals, at the ends of pews, or in pew racks. If there is also a printed weekly bulletin in the back of the church, it may contain some additional information about the service for the day. Most people who attend are, of course, members of the congregation; they know where to find helps for worship. If the priest has not taken the time to prepare a more detailed guide for worshipping, please do not blame him. Catholic priests are among the most overworked human beings in the world. In any case, a second visit to a church should leave you quite prepared to follow the service. For many reasons, you should give the Catholic Church a fair chance.

Perhaps I should add that, to a Catholic, Christ Himself is present during the service of worship. In most churches, in our invocation, we ask for God's presence among us, but Catholics seem to give more emphasis to this idea than other churches do.

Personal Lives

It is possible for any Christian to have a direct relationship with God through prayer. Many do. How many is known only to God. But in each of the three major branches of Christianity in the United States there are books to guide one's prayer life, and some members of churches get together for joint prayer. We should remember this whenever we estimate the total value of any church in the community, for this kind of prayer is often private or semi-private, and its importance may be very great to God. Incidentally, nowadays Catholics do not always say formal, prepared prayers only; they do pray in their own words, either alone or in small groups, sometimes groups that include a variety of Christian denominations.

Many of us ask Gods blessing before each meal, and often that occasion is used also as an occasion for praise, thanksgiving, even confession. Some Christians pray regularly at other times of day, as well, on waking in the morning, on retiring at night, and when about to start on a difficult task.

In every denomination we visited, there was some sort of devotional booklet, too, usually with a scripture, a commentary on the passage of scripture, and suggestions for prayers for that day.

Sometimes individual Christians within the various churches participate in worship services other than on Sunday morning. When I was young, the midweek prayer meeting at many churches was a standard, and I knew Catholics who went to mass every morning. Some churches still have services during the week, and, although there may be other people present, attending these services can be a part of one's personal worship, just as attending weeknight Bible study and prayer groups can be.

For some Christians, the daily study of a devotional booklet, plus the Sunday sermon, may be all of the time given to the serious acquisition of religious knowledge. Others attend Sunday School classes for adults on Sunday; as a retired teacher, I have been very much disappointed with most of these classes, however, this may not be the moment to express my personal feelings about what I deem to be their weaknesses.

A few people in any church group read popular books on religion. Very few, however, really study the types of books that would be used in seminaries in their denomination. — I know very well that one can have a great deal of knowledge about religion without applying its lessons to life; I know also that one can live the life of a good Christian without having much detailed knowledge that could not be acquired in a confirmation class or a Sunday School class for fourteen-year-olds. I know. But I do not know of any good reason for not studying one's religion, just as one would take the time to read the latest difficult books about one's profession or even about one's principal hobby. — We do not study our religion enough; that is true, however, of Roman Catholics, Mainline Protestants, and Conservative Protestants.

As to Christian service, there we are very much at fault. It is so easy to think of ourselves and be comfortable. To spend time with neighbors in distress, particularly with people who are not like ourselves, is likely to pose problems that could cause other problems for us; pretty soon, all of our time would be spent in helping others in our community. So we have turned the problem of helping others over to the government, haven't we? Oh, yes: We bake cookies, paint the church walls, sit in committee meetings and board meetings, and raise money to take care of the needs of our own local church. Anything more than these activities, though, involves risk. Human beings who are members of the three main branches of Christianity are alike: They are human, and, like people outside the church — almost as bad, but not quite, in my opinion — they look out for themselves, leaving little time for looking out for other people. — No denomination teaches selfishness; it is just the way we are as human beings.

Sources of Doctrine

Many Protestants feel that there can be only one source of church doctrine, the Bible. Yet even in Protestant churches that make this claim there are collective agreements about specific interpretations of the Bible. Nevertheless, we can honestly say that Catholics and Episcopalians do not say that their only source of doctrine is scripture; they add two other sources, tradition and reason.

Tradition would include whatever the denomination has done in the past, as evaluated by the powers of the present. Hence, the interpretations of scripture written by long-departed saints would be considered today. So would the customs of the past as applied to Christian worship, study, and service.

Reasons could include such processes as the system of logic espoused by St. Thomas Aquinas in the thirteenth century and by his successors. It could also include the systems of thought promoted by the Deists in the eighteenth century. And all of these, plus all theological propositions, past and recent, could be assessed by the rational processes of modern theologians and scholars.

Whether we admit it or not, and whether we think it is a good idea or not, all Christian denominators today base their doctrines on these three sources; some use one source more than others, however.

Power

Power sounds like a dirty word. Maybe it is. Lord Acton may well have been correct when he said that power corrupts. In my opinion, there is no perfect solution to the problem of power. Yet it seems to be necessary in the churches and the denominations. In theory, at least, power is wielded in the church in one of the following ways: by an authority figure, sometimes turning to advisers; by various authority figures, sometimes meeting together in parliament; by a parliament of some sort, usually with subordinate parliaments and usually advised by various committees and bureaucrats; by a local pastor, sometimes guided by, controlled by, or subject to censure by a church board; by a congregation of Christians; or by each individual Christian.

There are problems with each of these methods. I can think of at least one problem of some magnitude that is in part caused by each of the above methods. Having had some experience with denominations that professed each of these methods, I am not judging them as an outsider. — I should add that my experience has led me to respect some of the good things about each of these methods, too.

If one has power, one is tempted to use it, then use it some more, finally overuse it; that is, abuse it. I think that is what Lord Acton meant when he said that power corrupts. If each of us could be resigned to be a Christian; that is, a follower of Christ, there might be fewer problems. Most of us do not know how to put on the brakes, though, how to avoid substituting ourselves and our minds and wills for the mind and will of God. We lack humility; we permit our own egos to take control, and we become selfish, self-centered, jealous of the prerogatives of others, vengeful, vindictive, and full of hate for others. — That is what happens to all of us when we have power.

I can think of a dozen or more statements by Christians who have observed the use of power within their different church structures; generally their observations have a wistful note: They truly wish that power were not such a temptation for Christians who have it. But all of them have observed the abuse of power. So my opinions are not different from those of other observers.

Nevertheless, I know also that it is impossible to live a Christian life in isolation from other people who are making the same attempt. With all its foolishness, much of it caused by the abuse of power, some institutional church is necessary for us to survive as Christians.

Miscellaneous Differences

There are some differences between the churches in the three main branches of Christianity in America that I have not covered here, and one denomination differs from another in certain ways that I consider to be minor. For some serious inquirers, the official denominational restrictions on the individual's daily life may be a problem. You will do well to consider those before you decide to join a particular church.

These vary from one denomination to another, so your best way of finding out about them is simply to ask a pastor what the membership requirements are in his or her church, then follow that question up by asking what other restrictions on daily life are generally expected of church members. Be sure to take some time in discovering the answer, for rules governing the daily life of a church member are sometimes unstated, yet generally accepted.

The pastor of one Free Methodist church told me in an interview that all prospective members were asked to promise not to smoke, drink, or gamble. In some other churches these rules are not stated, but they are under-stood to be the case.

The Roman Catholic Church has what some have termed different levels of Christians. For all, as I understand it, certain days are considered to be fast days, certain worship services are required, and certain rules govern preparation for communion. But religious orders sometimes require the members of those orders to take vows of poverty, chastity, and obedience so as to forego the chief temptations of human life. Some priests are 'in the world,' some in religious orders, some in contemplative orders, and so on. Nuns also have their special rules and special vows.

Some denominations claim to have no creeds; yet they have almost universal local covenants not to drink alcoholic beverages. Some denominations officially leave this and other practices up to the conscience of the individual Christian; yet they do not consider anyone who drinks or smokes to be a good Christian.

You may have no problem with any of this, but you should be forewarned. In all of the three branches of Christianity, you may encounter some unfortunate surprises if you do not investigate in advance. Because Christian meaning should be present in all human lives, I believe, it would be sad for you to miss this meaning in your own life simply because you have not asked enough questions before joining a particular Christian church.

There is some Christian church that will fit your individual needs and your personality. You just have to take the time to find it.

CHAPTER THREE
CHOOSING A PASTOR

All of the differences between major divisions of Christianity may be very important to the individual who seeks serious Christian meaning for his or her life. Although they have been described in general terms in the preceding chapter, the importance of specific differences will depend upon the individual seeker: personal comfort and attitude toward style of worship, degree of independence and resistance to or acceptance of externally-imposed power, and so forth. Only you, the investigator, can really decide what you want and what you are most likely to feel comfortable and satisfied with. I would recommend that you give a number of different types of Christian church a try though; two visits would be more fair wherever you find some aspects of the denomination attractive, perhaps visits to two or more individual churches of the particular denomination.

But at least the second most important decision you make will be your choice of pastor. It may even be the most important.

There is an irony in this statement, for pastors do move from one church to another, usually within a particular denomination; the pastor you choose may not be your pastor for even the year or two you need to make a substantial entry upon a Christian life. On the other hand, wherever a local church has some influence on the selection of its next pastor, there tends to be a certain similarity in the pastors who serve that church. And in all of the denominations I know about, including Catholic, Episcopal, and Methodist, where a bishop makes the official appointment of the pastor, the local church is able to influence the choice of the new pastor. In most cases, you need not fear a dramatic change for the worse — the worse as far as you are concerned. If you like the present pastor, you probably will like the successor.

Is the Pastor a Christian?

We should not expect to find a pastor who is perfect, for all pastors are human beings. It is possible that most pastors once had some goal of living the Christian life, but pastors are almost universally overworked, and people who have more responsibilities than they can handle are likely to get to the point where they lose sight of the goals they once had. Different pastors start out their work lives with a variety of aims, of course, and there is no simple summary of what it is to be a Christian — that is, not one that would satisfy every person who seeks the

Christian life. Yet you may wish to apply some sort of simple checklist to the person you are considering as your possible guide for Christian living. So long as you do not expect the impossible; that is, so long as you know that there is no perfect Christian, I suggest that you measure each pastor you encounter more or less on the basis of the standards outlined by Dr. Walter Russell Bowie in his article on the parables in Volume VII of **The Interpreters Bible**. In that article, he says that Jesus taught that His disciples would display the following marks: humility, the spirit of forgiveness, the recognition of duty, sympathy, true neighborliness, and the love of God.

The standards Bowie identifies are indeed high ones. I do know some pastors who exhibit these qualities in their daily lives, in their understanding of what Christ taught, and in their teaching and preaching. I believe that I could identify most of these persons in two visits to their churches. I know all too well how easily I can be fooled, of course, but these qualities are difficult to fake even at a distance. They are worth keeping in mind as you visit churches.

Now, how, you might ask, can a pastor not be a Christian?

Easy: The world outside the church — and outside the New Testament, as well — bombards us all daily with slogans that are contradictory, in my opinion, to the teachings of Christ. Future pastors, student pastors, the teachers of future pastors and student pastors, and beginning pastors themselves are all very much aware of these slogans. Sometimes the difference is a matter of method; for example, one may seek to bring about a goal that is compatible with what Christ sets as a standard, yet use worldly methods of achieving such a goal. Sometimes it is a result of an erratic study of the goals Christ has set for us; without offending too many Christians, perhaps I may offer as an example of this type of misplaced energy the pastor's concentration on a kind of reform more often discussed in sociology classes than in seminary classes in religion. — But the world presses in on us all the time.

I do not wish to blame the spouse and children, if any, for the sins of the pastor, the pastor's departures from the Christian code in favor of the worldly code of success; but of course the pastor, if given a choice between two paths, may sometimes take the one that leads to financial security for the entire family, including self. I live reasonably well in retirement, for example. Most of the younger people in our Presbyterian church — or, for that matter, in most churches in our larger community — do well, too. Since the end of World War II, we have had a period of relative prosperity, perhaps the longest period of its type in world history. Americans live well. It is natural, then, that pastors and their families wish to live well, also. — Not as well as I do, perhaps, but they do wish **to make sure that when everyone else around them seems to be comfortable they do not deny** that privilege to spouse and children — and themselves.

Once again, you say, 'How can a pastor not be a Christian?' After all, if the pastor just says the right words, but does not model them for the congregation, the lessons will not be learned. — Sometimes we simply need to be content to have the pastor say the right words. The pastor may be on her or his way to becoming a Christian without having reached close to the goal as yet.

With respect to this last statement, I should explain that in looking over my own life, I have discovered that although I have known the right words for many years, I have not put them into practice completely, and probably I am not yet sufficiently self-critical to have eliminated my own worst faults, my failures as a Christian. Why should I expect a pastor to have done more?

Look for a Christian pastor. Do not expect to find one who has gone all the way. But look for someone who seems to preach at himself or herself as well as to the peo ple in the congregation; that is, at least, one sign that the pastor is still capable of self-criticism.

Believe it or not, there are many Christian pastors out there, pastors of all ages. They are humble, forgiving, sympathetic to others, good neighbors, and full of love for God. I have met many of them, and you will, too, if you look with an open mind and heart and if you apply your critical skills to yourself as well as to those around you.

What to Look For

From what I have said above, you may conclude that the bachelor priest of the Roman Catholic Church makes the ideal pastor. Sometimes he does, but not always, and not in every way. For one thing, the typical priest has far too much to do; there are just not enough priests to shepherd all of the flocks adequately, though most of those in the field make a brave attempt to do so. And while the priest may not have to worry about the needs of spouse or children, the priest does not have the day-to-day experience of living in a family group, experience that can make the Protestant pastor better able to understand the conflicting tugs of a family member's will. There are priests who are unable to deal successfully with sex, of course, just as there are Protestant pastors who cannot do that well. In theory, the Catholic priest is often a good pastor; about equally, I believe the Protestant pastor may be, as well. I would not advise the seeker to choose one or the other simply because of the pastor's family situation.

The following suggestions may help you find the right pastor:

1. Seek out a pastor who is a good listener. Not everyone is, even though he or she knows the right words to say.

2. Look for a pastor who seeks to find God's intent in His scriptures, not necessarily for a pastor who is absolutely sure of God's meaning. — Such a pastor may have made the regrettable leap from attempting to discover God's mind to knowing what is there; that is, he or she may have slipped into self-worship, often without knowing it.

3. At the risk of repeating what I have already said, look for a pastor who is trying to become a Christian and who includes self in the group to whom his or her sermons are directed.

4. Expect the pastor to be aware of what we call 'opportunities for advancement,' but do not choose a pastor whose main concern is 'getting ahead.' If you have time, read the little book by Charles Merrill Smith entitled **How to Become Bishop Without Being Religious**, by a bishop.)

This checklist could go on and on, but those four points should be enough to keep you from going far astray.

A Final Note

In interviewing twenty pastors, representing the various denominations we had visited in our research, I asked questions prepared in advance. The following answers were given either by all twenty or by almost all:

A typical work week for a pastor is sixty hours in length. Some work longer than that, and most of them work as many as eighty hours in their busiest weeks of the year.

There is almost always a considerable gap between the religious knowledge of the pastor and the religious knowledge of the average church member. In a large majority of cases, this gap also exists between pastor and members of the church boards. The pastor, then, is usually the one person in the church unit (unless there are two or more pastors) who has a relatively complete understanding of Christianity.

In spite of the tremendous time pressures on pastors, every pastor I interviewed said that if a serious seeker after Christian meaning for life asked for instruction, he or she would provide that instruction on a one-to-one basis if necessary. (In a few cases, the pastor regularly taught a class for adult inquirers during the Sunday School hour.)

In spite of the many frustrations of the pastorate, ninety-five percent of those pastors interviewed said that, if starting out again, they would become pastors rather than some other sort of professional, and would choose the denomination in which they presently served. Even the one pastor (five percent of twenty) who said he might have chosen another vocation if he were to do it over again, said that he might also have become a pastor; he simply wasn't sure.

Pastors are very important to every member of every church; as a profession, they deserve our respect and understanding.

CHAPTER FOUR
HOW BIG A CHURCH SHOULD BE

In our one hundred visits to churches on Sunday mornings, we attended one church that claimed to have twelve thousand members and one that had only a dozen present at its single Sunday morning service. The average number of members in local churches belonging to the standard denominations is probably around two hundred to three hundred.

Why should the number of members in a church be important for you? Because what your needs are as a human being will be about as much affected by the size of the church as any other factor — except for denomination and pastor, which we have already spoken about.

Some authorities on 'successful churches' recommend what they call the megachurch, claiming that it is the way churches will go in the future. There is something in this conclusion. As they point out, a church of, say, two or three thousand members, can often afford to provide special interest groups to meet the needs of all ages and all interest levels likely to be found in a church community. Large churches can also provide a staff of professionals who can specialize in one or more of the following concerns: preaching, music, Christian education, youth work, counseling, visitation, business administration, community outreach, and so forth. Such a large church can also maintain a large clerical staff, a bright, shiny kitchen, a substantial recreation program, and a well-supervised custodial staff.

All of that is correct. I have been a member of congregations as large as thirteen hundred and as small as seventy, and I have served individual churches as pastor that had no more than thirty-five persons present at their biggest services. I can agree with all of the plaudits given to the very large churches. They tend to be the models for teachers and students in seminaries to discuss.

They have one other distinct attraction for inquirers: A new person, even after joining such a church, can retain a certain degree of anonymity; and many inquirers find this to be a blessing. I can understand that.

But when I interviewed twenty pastors who were doing a good job in their churches, most of them said that the ideal church size was about four hundred. Some of them, now in much larger churches, said it wistfully. — I should add that I did not include Roman Catholic churches in this chapter; although they have many qualities that should appeal to the serious inquirer, they are, as a group, afflicted by a severe shortage of priests. Almost all Catholic churches that I know about are large by Protestant standards of membership, and few of them have more than one priest to serve their hundreds of parishioners. Four hundred as the ideal church size. That deserves some discussion, for the pastors interviewed were experts, most of them with long years of service behind them.

A congregation of four hundred members is large enough to pay the pastor's salary without too much anxiety, and to pay a full-time secretary to relieve the pastor from certain nonprofessional duties and to pay a custodian well enough to keep the building in good shape. In addition, the pastor will be able to know well, after a reasonable length of time, all of the members of the congregation, their nonmember children, and even many of their relatives in other churches in the community. — All of this knowledge makes it possible for the pastor to preach more relevant sermons to his congregation, make informed visits to persons who are ill or in distress, and take the responsibility for being a wise older cousin at times of grief for the family.

Most pastors who are good at their jobs are conscientious persons; they want to do everything their parishioners expect of them, and parishioners invariably expect the pastor of their church to know who they are. In a church with four hundred members, the pastor can do that.

Some pastors interviewed believe that they would be able to serve a parish of as many as six hundred without having anyone but a full-time secretary to help out. One pastor recalled having served a parish of nine hundred and felt that he had done a good job there. But four hundred is a typical maximum size. Some who were interviewed said they felt that a church they had served with only about two hundred members represented the most satisfying time in their careers. — Oddly enough, the average church in Protestantism is between two and three hundred in size.

Yet seminary classes often discuss what to do in a truly 'successful' church of over a thousand members. Since the majority of pastors will have churches of three hundred or fewer persons, at least in their early years in the pastorate, the seminary discussions of much larger churches than that do two things that are bad: First, they assume that somehow every congregation should try to imitate the big ones and feel that they are failures if they cannot have all of the programs and possibilities one can find in a large church. Second, the very real possibilities of churches of average size may be neglected in seminary analyses. And in the church of average size, there is a potential for it to be an extended family, a quality lacking in very big congregations.

Now, what could be wrong with a megachurch? Remember that it is recommended by a number of authorities on what kind of church is truly successful.

There is invariably a distance between pastor and people. I have seen pastors make valiant efforts to give large congregations the feeling of belonging to the church, but nothing has been completely satisfactory. In one church of more than a thousand, each of us elders was assigned one twelfth of the congregation to 'pastor.' Each of us held a meeting at his or her home, with the pastor present, and about half the number on our list for shepherding showed up; but the attempt soon ceased, and we went back to the situation before, when the pastor had attempted to learn something about all of our members. In another church of thirteen hundred members, we called a new pastor for the first time in over fifteen years. He did have an associate pastor who had been on the scene for three years, a part-time youth director, and two secretaries, one of whom really knew everyone in the con gregation. But the new pastor wanted to get acquainted right away with everyone in the congregation. We had question and answer meetings with him in various homes, about twenty in each group. It served some purpose, but the energy expended and the number of nights the pastor had to give to the task made that effort stop, too.

The point is, that a big church would like to have the natural potential of a church of average size, even though the average church thinks of the very large church as successful.

Now, I have known of congregations of twenty-five hundred served by five full-time, fully-ordained pastors, one, of course, being the senior pastor, each of the others more specialized. What is wrong with such an arrangement? It sounds as though such a church would be large enough to do everything for everybody, a supposed advantage of large churches. In addition, one could divide the five pastors into the twenty-five hundred people and require each pastor to learn only five hundred individuals; surely that would be an achievable goal. Here is the problem: Each of the pastors, for his or her specialty, has to know all twenty-five hundred members of the congregation. Think about that for a time, and you'll understand what I mean: The person preaching cannot preach just to the five hundred she or he knows; the counselor must expect to have to counsel any of the twenty-five hundred persons in the congregation. And so on.

I have a dozen or so stories I could tell about the problems of a large church, many of them humorous, a few very, very sad, shocking in a tragic way. As a former pastor, I know how important it is to know as much as possible about every person in the church; once in a great while, that knowledge can be a matter of life and death. So I can see why most of the twenty pastors I interviewed felt that a congregation of four hundred was just right.

But that is still a matter for you to decide about. There are no perfect human beings and no perfect churches. My best experiences as a human being trying to be a Christian were in churches of fewer than five hundred persons. But so were two experiences that would be enough to send a tentative inquirer running away from Christianity.

Church size is not the only consideration, not by any means; but it does deserve your careful attention.

I Have a dozen or so stories I could tell about the problems of a large church, many of them humorous, a few very, very sad, shocking in a tragic way. As a former pastor, I know how important it is to know as much as possible about every person in the church; once in a great while, that knowledge can be a matter of life and death. So I can see why most of the twenty pastors I interviewed felt that a congregation of four hundred was just right.

CHAPTER FIVE
THE BEST CHURCH STRUCTURE FOR YOU

A columnist for the **Des Moines Register** in the 1950's, a man named Harlan Miller, probably more famous for his regular column in **Better Homes and Gardens** called, I believe, 'There's A Man Around the House,' and best known to the world-wide public, though anonymously, as the in spiration for the reporter in the movie **State Fair** repeated many times in his column an enigmatic statement that I often quoted to my English classes as a guide to scholarship in the humanities: 'There is no solution. Seek it lovingly.'

Harlan Miller's statement applies not only to research in the humanities, but also to certain matters of human attempts to practice Christianity. Human beings — you and I — are imperfect, subject to what Paul calls the temptations of the flesh. I substitute the word **world** but I think we mean the same: Whenever human beings start out to do anything, they react from habit, habit acquired in their worldly pursuits. And one of our most difficult lusts to contend with is the lust for power over people. Closely related to that in many cases is the lust for status — that is, to have position and reputation in the eyes of other **people**. (The contrast is between reputation in the eyes of people and known character in the eyes of God, who sees all.)

Remember, I believe in the existence of something commonly called the devil. Perhaps it is simply the sin that dwells within us, as Paul occasionally refers to our impulse to do the wrong thing. Whatever it is, and whatever others may call it, I believe that this impulse to ignore the promptings we find in the New Testament is a factor we should always consider. Remember, we see it most in others, but we surely must know that it is in ourselves, as well. For example, I recently read of the retirement of a pastor who was supposedly known for his great humility. Now, I have known many truly humble persons, including pastors; but I had had one encounter with the man in question, and that incident had left me with the impression that the man was far more proud and arrogant than most of us are. I have read newspaper reports about two different persons who advised everyone to develop an atmosphere of trust; in each case, although I recognized certain admirable qualities in the individual, my own experiences with them had taught me never to trust either of them. — In my own case, I tend to believe that my goal is to follow the principles set for the Christian life in the New Testament; yet I know that some of my acquaintances, even my wife, discern deep **faults** in me. (I doubt if I should ever write an article advising others to temper **their** inclination to be aggressive or assertive or independent, for examples. I'm **sure** I have worse faults than those, even.)

All of this is prologue: In **Matthew 16:14-19**, we encounter the narrative of Christ's establishment of His church on earth, a passage whose interpretation has been aggressively and violently disputed by Catholics and Protestants.

Catholics say that this passage means that Peter himself is the foundation of the church. Peter became, we are told, the first bishop of Rome, and all subsequent bishops of Rome (popes) have been regarded by Catholics as the head of their church.

Protestants generally point out that later chapters in the same Gospel give details of Peter's imperfect humanity: his violent use of a sword, for example; his apparent weakness of will in assuring Christ that he, Peter, will be loyal always, then denying Him three times in a few hours, as Jesus had told him he would. — How could such a man as Peter become the head of Christ's church on earth, they ask. Instead, many Protestants consider Peter's confession ('Thou art the Christ, the Son of the Living God') as being the foundation of the church on earth; in other words, Christ's true church is made up of all of those who share in Peter's confession.

church on earth; in other words, Christ's true church is made up of all of those who share in Peter's confession.

Both of these interpretations make sense to me. I would not care to participate in burning at the stake anyone who took one interpretation or the other, but — admit ting, as most church confessions do, that each of us as a human being is imperfect, incapable of knowing the entire mind of God — I can see how either approach could guide Christian people in the conduct of Christ's church on earth.

There is another tradition, quite old, but not much talked about today, that Christ founded His church on the **kind** of Christian that Peter was. This also makes sense to me. I have never met a perfect Christian, including myself, and I do know that complacency is one of the great enemies of those attempting to practice the Christian life; yet I know, too, that churches have existed for thousands of years and that they have served various useful and important purposes, in spite of the fact that they have not been perfect.

It is very important, I believe, to belong to a church. Some are closer to the New Testament than others, in my opinion. But none of them is perfect; nor should we expect to find a perfect church. Human beings have tended to organize churches on one of the following three plans: the authoritarian system, the parliamentary system, and the congregational system. Each of them has good points, and each of them has bad. In the following pages, I shall attempt to offer you a guide to both the values and the hazards of these three basic types of church structure.

The Authoritarian System

Provided that all concerned in either system are working hard at being Christians, the authoritarian system can, I believe, be the best way of appointing pastors to flocks. Inasmuch as the persons with authority are experts in religion, they should be able to make wise decisions with regard to the interpretation of the holy scriptures, of tradition, and of what reason says is right. If the mass of Christians in the churches are unwilling to study religion and seek an easy way out, then the easier way is to follow the instructions of experts: to fast when the experts say they should fast, to attend worship services when they say they should, to teach their children and conduct family life as the authorities say they should, and even to vote as they are told by authorities with power and with expert knowledge.

All of this makes sense, I believe. On the other hand, having power tends to make the possessors of power careless of the outcomes of their use of power. Whatever checks and balances exist do not always prevent tragic results. A major question: Does any one individual have the right to make a decision that affects for better or worse the relationship between God and the individual Christian? Many Catholics, for example, believe that it is the right of the priest or bishop to make such a decision. That is a part of the Catholic tradition. But many Protestants feel much the same, and they treat their pastors or higher committees or bureaucrats and officials within their denominations in about the same way that devout Catholics supposedly treat their priests: as they would treat plumbers, electricians, lawyers, or medical doctors. In this day of turning to specialists for technical work, it is natural that Protestants, particularly those who do not wish to study and learn religion on their own, may want their pastors to become priests, and so on. And power corrupting, as Lord Acton said it did, it is a great temptation for pastors to accept the role of priests, even though their supposedly expert knowledge of the Protestant tradition should tell them not to.

The Catholic way of authority has its own logic, in my opinion. It offers a reasonable alternative to the other two basic church structures, for each of them has its flaws. But my own opinion is that any Protestant who wants the pastor to act in the role of a priest is lazy and that any Protestant pastor who accepts that role is fundamentally dishonest. If I wished to be a part of an authoritarian

101

system, I would choose the Catholic Church. In that organization, there is enough experience with the mistakes of authority for bishops and such to be on their guard, ready to remove or transfer a priest who has yielded too much to the temptation of power. In Protestant churches, there is no corrective system in place, and a great many people may suffer and/or become disenchanted with Christianity when a Protestant pastor takes over the role of priest.

Luther and the other early reformers pointed out some of the dangers of the Roman Catholic system. Modern Catholics admit that there have been bad popes, bad bishops, and bad priests. Luther and others pointed out the wrongs created by the sale of indulgences — as though the Pope or bishops or priests could speak and act completely for God. The Protestant reformation created churches that operated either on the parliamentary or the congregational system of theological interpretation and that attempted to place responsibility for the health of the individual soul squarely on the individual self. That is quite different from the authoritarian tradition.

We should remember that other denominations than the Roman Catholic Church use the authoritarian system or some variation of it. The Eastern Orthodox churches do, I am told, and so does the Episcopal Church in the United States. Springing from the Episcopal Church, the United Methodist Church, as well as many smaller groups, has its system of bishops, cloaked with some of the kinds of authori ty of Roman Catholic and Episcopal bishops. The Methodist churches, however, have regional, state, and national conferences that utilize some aspects of the parliamentary system; but bishops appoint, transfer, and remove from office pastors in the Methodist churches.

As I have probably suggested already, the two major problems with the authoritarian system are that someone or some group would seem to come between the in dividual soul and God and that those with power are tempted to abuse it.

The Parliamentary System

Many denominations use the parliamentary system to degree. That is, some authoritarian systems develop advisory groups, and some essentially congregational denominations develop systems of parliamentary assemblies. Particularly in the United States. Americans seem to love to get together as representatives of something and, whenever possible, pass resolutions. The resolutions we pass at such assemblies may be misinterpreted by members of other denominations who read the newspaper reports of the meetings, and they are sometimes misinterpreted by the reporters who write the accounts. How much authority does the resolution passed by a particular assembly have? Sometimes the answer is buried in one or more complex constitutions. Sometimes not even the majority of persons attending an assembly really know how much weight their resolutions carry.

I am a member of the Presbyterian Church. That denomination is very proud of the fact that its system of government had much influence on the development of the system of government originally adopted by the United States of America. — Having said as much, I must admit that holders of political office in the United States today are not regarded with wholehearted esteem. We know that they are frequently guilty of compromise, failure to study accurately and carefully lengthy committee reports that recommend legislation to be passed, horse trading on various issues, giving too much power to bureaucrats and to persons with important posts, trendiness (at the expense of calm, considered decisions), fear of pressure groups, and overresponse to special interest groups. — Well, most persons elected to local church sessions (boards), meetings of Presbytery, meetings of Synods and meetings of the General Assembly are honest, more so than the average, I am sure. Otherwise, they have the same problems that I have listed for members of the United States Congress. They, too, like to pass resolutions, and those they pass have some force, unlike those usually passed by assemblies of denominations that are essentially congregational in nature. For instead of a Pope or a Presiding Bishop, the Presbyterians have no higher authority than the General Assembly. In other words, when the General Assembly speaks, it is, in effect, interpreting the mind of God.

The mind Of God!

Hans Kung , a Catholic theologian, has pointed out the problem of compromise among experts (bishops in that case) about what is in the mind of God. One famous meeting of experts (bishops) in the early centuries of Christianity met to debate the issue of whether or not woman had a soul. Their decision was in the affirmative, but only by one vote out of about sixty bishops present. For one thing, I wonder just how valuable was the expert knowledge of the dissenting bishops. For another, I wonder how history might have been changed if two of the bishops voting in the affirmative had been absent that day.

I do not have much respect for the parliamentary system, whether the representatives voting are experts in the subject or nonexperts. And as a member of the session (an active elder) in five different Presbyterian churches over the years, I have no reason at all to believe that the Presbyterian parliamentary system regularly speaks the mind of God. I am positive that it does not, and I could cite many reversals of decisions to make my case if I chose; but in this case, I shall skip the long digression.

103

The Presbyterians have what is supposedly the model of parliamentary government. For that reason, I have spent some time in explaining it. I should add that both ordained pastors and ordinary laypersons ordained as elders in their churches take part in the various elected bodies; I might also add that the laypersons who serve as elders very seldom have made an extensive study of their religion or of the Christian religion.

So what are the alternatives? The authoritarian system described above and the congregational system I shall attempt to describe below.

The Congregational System

I have already pointed out that most denominations have assemblies or conventions of some sort, even when those meetings have no authority over the individual local churches in the denomination. The most highly organized denomination of independent churches I know about is the huge Southern Baptist Church, the largest Protestant denomination in the United States. It has no creed; yet each local church may, if it chooses, adopt a covenant to govern the religious and personal lives of its own members. Many of these covenants are alike; yet they are not forced on the local churches from higher up; I know of one or more Southern Baptist churches that do not prohibit the drinking of alcoholic beverages, for example, though many of the churches in the denomination do.

A major problem of churches organized on the congregational system is their inability to support missions, seminaries, colleges, and other institutions other than through individual local efforts. The Southern Baptist Church does unite in the support of seminaries, one or more publishing houses, missions, and colleges, at least to some extent; but the local churches remain independent in their super vision of their own members. — That is the way I understand it, at least.

The independent Christian church, a Campbellite church, in which I grew up supports missions through direct giving to individual missionaries. Yet many of its member churches subscribe to the church publications of a single publishing house, and the churches of that denomination do send delegates to periodic conventions of the church.

Some independent churches do not cooperate with other churches for any purpose at all. Generally conser vative, their pastors are graduates of colleges and seminaries supported by other churches or of public institutions.

Now, what is it like to belong to a church that is independent?

First of all, we should point out that churches organized along the congregational lines include various social classes. So do churches with either authoritarian or parliamentary structures. When I was a child, the three most aristocratic churches in my home town were the Episcopal, the Congregational, and the Presbyterian. I could also name certain churches in each structural group that were made up largely of members of the lower classes in my community. The Congregational Church in Quincy, Illinois, where I grew up, did not take part in the merger with the Evangelical churches that produced the United Church of Christ nationally. Neither did some other Congregational churches choose to merge.

The local church board, sometimes with recommendations from the pastor, has complete authority in a completely independent church. That board is made up of persons who have not studied religion at the college or seminary level — in almost every case. Often their knowledge of religion comes from the local Sunday School and from home study of the Bible. I am sorry to say that even such study is not as serious as it was in, say, the early 1800's. The members of the board sometimes have greater religious knowledge than do the members of a Presbyterian session (board), but they still do not know much about even the scriptures. Few of them would claim to be experts in religion. Yet the members of that board, elected by the congregation and sometimes subject to congregational oversight, can make rules to govern the conduct of the members of the entire congregation and can render to all members of the church what they believe God thinks about any issue.

I have not made the congregational kind of church sound attractive, I am sure. Nor have I made either the parliamentary style or the authoritarian style sound appealing. In a way, that is unfortunate, for I know of many churches in every structure that it would be a pleasure to belong to. But their structures are not particularly calculated to be of much help to the serious seeker of Christian meaning for life. Sorry—that's the way it is.

You Take Your Choice

Church structure is important because it tells us where the power is in the church. Human beings have great difficulty in coping with power. Most of all, they have trouble in deciding what God wants; yet they are eager to pass resolutions or to wield office or power in churches as though there were no problems involved.

You must make your own choice, of course. But be alert to the problems built into different church structures. Look out for power abusers. They may be pastors, priests, elders, deacons, congregational political leaders, or whatever. But the lust for power is always around, ready to destroy any church.

Yet, in spite of all of this, I believe that every human being should be a member of a Christian church. There are, however, many factors to consider when choosing that church. In the next chapter, I'll try to review some of those factors.

Incidentally, if I were starting out church life again, knowing what I know now, I would attend church regularly, but I would never serve on a church board.

God bless you.

CHAPTER SIX
CHECKLIST FOR VISITING CHURCHES

It is very, very important to be careful in choosing a church. Yet it is very, very easy to just let it happen to us. Almost any church can seem appealing to most of us if we do not go about our search in a systematic way, particularly we rely just on a few visits to a single local church. I believe that there is probably a satisfactory Christian church for every human being on earth; yet I also know that almost every individual human being could be repelled by some aspects of many churches, in the United States, at least. (I suspect, in the rest of the world, as well.)

There is in America a strong movement toward unity among the many (more than 250) denominations. Perhaps God does want the churches to work together more closely than they have in the past. On the other hand, it may be God's intent that there be as many different types of churches as there are types of human needs. We cannot know that, of course; nor can we know that God wants us to have no choice, that the human beings in power in one denomination, say, have discovered precisely what is in God's mind, and that whatever statement of theology and order of worship that group of human beings arrives at must, therefore, truly represent what God would have us think and do. — I personally cannot place that much trust in the imperfect human mind; my own study of history does not warrant such trust. Because I do not believe in the perfection of any human beings including those who are expert in religious matters, I cannot be much concerned about the campaigns for Christian church unity. Wise human beings often recommend them, so I may very well be wrong; but I do believe that there is a chance that God approves some of our present differences in churches, mainly because each individual human being is different and understands ideas in different ways.

Some Comparable Decisions We Make

Our lives are full of decisions, a few of them very important, others not so likely to change much about our individual world. Some decisions, however, can and do make a major difference in our ways of living and thinking. Among these are our decisions about marriage and children, about our careers, about our education, and about where and in what kind of housing we want to live. — Some would add the kinds of cars we drive. —More important than any of these, however, is our decision about religion. It is also our decision about where and how to find happiness in life, so it affects all of the other decisions, too. If, for example, we decide to marry a particular human being, marriage counselors tell us that the marriage will be happy or unhappy depending on how well we can agree on five or six subjects, one of which is religion. Our religious beliefs, then, can affect our decision about marriage.

The career we choose to follow will also be affected by our religious decision. Jesus tells us that we cannot serve God and Mammon, for one of them will take precedence over the other. As I understand that statement, we may be in business, of course, but our commitment will be to Christ, not to the pursuit of wealth. We cannot worship the stock market, say, as a god and our stockbroker as its priest. At the risk of sounding more narrow than I intend to sound, I must add that the largest single group of practicing Christians I ever worked with were teachers in an inner city junior high. That was in part an accident, I suppose, for I have seen and known about other groups of teachers at the elementary and secondary levels who were not so completely Christian in either their beliefs or their practices — nor, I should add, in their results. And at the college level, I have never encountered such a group of dedicated practicing Christians, though such groups may exist.

But I know that there are many other careers than teaching open to the devout Christian. I have known sincere practicing Christians who have been social workers, pastors, lawyers, elected officials, government workers, farmers, retailers, salespersons, factory workers and supervisors, and business executives of various sorts. I can name Christian plumbers, electricians, carpenters, librarians, and so forth. Sometimes the Christian chooses a particular kind of career in order to serve others. Sometimes the Christian simply decides to use Christian methods of doing whatever needs to be done in a particular career.

But the kind of career one chooses usually determines the nature of one's education, since most education is intended to prepare us for careers. Religion, then, is important in the other major decisions of our lives. We need to treat our religious decisions with caution and respect. Both qualities require us to take our time.

After all, we know how much emotion may be attached to falling in love and getting married. Yet even in making that decision, impulsive and emotional as it may sometimes be, most states have laws requiring us to give the decision a few days time. Conventional engagements often last for a number of months, sometimes even for more than a year, each party having the right up until the final step is taken in marriage, to back out of the arrangement.

I recommend that the search for a church take from three to six months of careful study. Remember, this decision is for life, and it affects all other important decisions.

Churches to Visit

In a three-month period, you can visit only twelve Sunday morning worship services, unless the churches on your list provide some alternatives, such as a Saturday mass, a Sunday evening service, or two services on Sunday morning. Even the very dedicated person, however, is not likely to be able to attend more than twenty or so regular worship services in a three-month period. I would suggest that much of the first three months be used for exploration and that the last three months be devoted to moving closer to a final decision. And if the decision really seems to require more than six months, it is better to take more time than to make the wrong decision. — On the other hand, one should work at this process intently, not just go to church now and then and put off making a decision.

In the exploratory phase of the search, I would suggest that the inquirer visit at least one church in each of the three major branches of Christianity two or more times. Such visits will tend to dispel some of the prejudices that most people have about certain denominations. Or so I believe.

Allowing for variations from community to community or from one part of America to another, I feel that your initial list of churches should be made up from something like the following selection of denominations:

Roman Catholic Churches: (Pretty much a category to themselves; if, however, you have grown up in an Eastern Orthodox church, you may wish to substitute a local church of that variety for the Roman Catholic.)

Mainline Protestant Churches: Although different in origin, the following denominations are usually included: United Methodist, Presbyterian, United Church of Christ, American Baptist, Disciples of Christ (Christian). As far as their approach to the scriptures is concerned, and largely with respect to theological conclusions, we may also include in this group the Evangelical Lutheran Churches and the Episcopal Church; both groups are likely to emphasize liturgy, however, so you may regard them as a separate group of Mainline Protestants.

Conservative Protestant Churches: Most of the more than 250 denominations in the United States fall into this group; Catholics are the largest single denomination in total numbers, but the Southern Baptists, almost a third as big as the Catholics, are a part of the conservative Protestant group.

Because there are so many denominations in this group, I shall simply list a few representatives: the Southern Baptists, the Nazarenes, the Free Methodists, the independent Christians, the Church of Christ (related to the independent Christians and to the Disciples of Christ (all Campbellites), the Christian Alliance churches, the other Baptist groups except for the American (northern) Baptists, the Christian Reformed churches (as distinct from the Reformed Churches, which are mainline), the Orthodox Presbyterians.

Three groups are conservative, but have marked distinctions from those named above. One is the Church of Latter Day Saints (two branches, the Mormons); they are conservative, but they add to the scriptures the Book of Mormon. (Catholics add what Protestants refer to as the Apocrypha; Episcopalians and Lutherans add liturgies that include scripture, but also include other items; many church groups, both mainline and conservative, as well as Catholics, give official status to certain ancient creeds. the Christian Science Church regards Eddy's book of commen tary as scripture.)

A quite distinct group is made up of what are called 'charismatics,' though individual charismatics may exist within any denomination. The specific denominations that are charismatic in nature, however, are the Assembly of God, the Holiness churches, and the Pentecostals. Most of the charismatics I have encountered outside these denominations belong to the Catholic, Methodist, Episcopal, and Presbyterian churches, none of which stress adult baptism. Charismatics are almost always conservative in their approach to scripture.

Lutherans are divided, I should add. Two synods of Lutherans are definitely conservative: the Missouri Synod (much larger than the name implies) and the Wisconsin Synod. Both use much the same liturgy as the Evangelical Lutherans do, but they are traditional in their Bible interpretation.

There are also completely independent churches, as well as independent Christian and independent Baptist institutions. Some of them call themselves Bible churches; usually they do not take part in larger efforts of Christian churches or in local ministerial associations.

A Sample List

You may use your telephone directory yellow pages (under Churches) to gain information about the denominations that are represented in your community. If I were you, thinking seriously about a church home, I would first visit churches at some distance from my home. It is natural and normal for Christians in any church group to welcome you, perhaps with greater effort than you want them to exhibit. (Remember, these are largely amateurs at the task; they are fumbling toward the right way to greet visitors, so be patient with them.) People in the next town are not likely to expect you to join their church, so churches twenty miles from your home are good to visit when you are simply asking yourself questions and trying to form conclusions that will be subject to change. Only after you have visited at least five churches at a distance, in my opinion, should you approach churches in your own neighborhood.

Because denomination presence's vary from one part of the country to another, I would suggest that you be prepared to substitute rather freely on the list below; but I believe it would be useful to visit one of each of the following in the first three months:

1. A working-class Roman Catholic Church.

2. A Roman Catholic Church in a 'nice' neighborhood.

3. A Lutheran Church. (Either Evangelical or Missouri Synod.)

4. A large United Methodist Church.

5. A smaller mainline Protestant Church (Presbyterian, Methodist, U.C.C., Disciples of Christ.)

6. A Southern Baptist Church.

7. A Church of God (or Free Methodist or Alliance or Nazarene.)

8. An independent Christian church.

9. An Assembly of God Church.

10. Another kind of conservative Protestant church: Covenant, Quaker, Christian Science, Bible church, LDS Church, etc.

Sometime in your first three or four months, it would be good to get the broad view of Christian churches that such visits would give you. After obtaining such a broad view, it is time to think about narrowing down your list, but not until then, in my opinion. You may find that some visits are complete 'turnoffs,' but you are almost sure to find some denominations with which you have rapport, in whose services you feel comfortable. This experience may show you how easy it is for adults to reject all Christian churches simply because of a few bad experiences in a narrow aspect of Christianity in their youth.

Using a Checklist

I would not advise you to go into a church with a checklist in hand. For one thing, it is not necessary. Instead, make sure you obtain the printed bulletin or other printed materials about the specific local church as well as any materials that seem relevant and that are on display in the church lobby about the denomination. (Be prepared to deposit a few coins for devotionals and so forth.)

But think through the checklist below before making a visit; then write down the answers as soon as reasonably possible after the visit.

1. How do I feel about this church as I look at it from the outside: parking lot, landscaping, building exterior, etc.?

2. How do I feel about the sanctuary (worship area) as I sit there quietly?

3. Does the music give me a feeling of peace and comfort, or does it irritate me? If it does, why?

4. Do the hymnals, worship aids, or materials projected on a screen or wall for the congregation to use help me to worship God? How? Or why not?

5. Do I feel that most of those present are truly worshipping?

6. Am I greeted by people, before and afterwards without their being nosy?

7. Do those assigned to platform tasks seem to know what they are doing?

8. Do I believe that I could trust the pastor?

9. Is the atmosphere of the church one of love or hate? If hate, what is the object of the hate, and how can hate be justified?

10. (If applicable.) Does the pastor seem willing to give me information about the denomination and the church?

Other Visits

I would not care to prescribe a visiting list for you; even what I have suggested is intended to be a sample, not a list to follow. But I do think that samples are useful and may save you time in planning your own program of visits.

Probably you will wish to begin narrowing down your own list after you have obtained a broad view of the forms Christianity takes in your area. Then, but still working with a list of four or five local churches in hand, try to learn a good deal about each of them and make at least three visits to at least four churches before you begin to settle on one. Let me give you an example: Although my first wife was a Presbyterian from Scotland and I had been in the Disciples of Christ denomination, there were two occasions in our several moves in which we did not find a local representative of either of these denominations. In one case, we visited the Methodist, the Congregational, the American Baptists and an independent Christian church before making up our minds. We attended each of them two or three times, felt generally comfortable worshipping in each of them, and finally made our decision because the pastor of one of them seemed to be about where we were on the conservative-liberal continuum and was also a person we could talk to. The second part was important, but not so much as the first. In another case, we chose a Presbyterian church in a nearby community, but first we visited an independent Christian, a United Methodist five miles away, a small United Methodist a mile away, and an Orthodox Presbyterian church about six miles away. In that instance, we considered denomination, distance, church size, and the pastors involved. We felt that we could have been comfortable in all of those we visited, but the one we finally chose was, we thought, somewhat superior in an overall way to the others. But if we had rushed to join any particular local church, we would have chosen one closer to home.

What factors would you consider in your Search? Review the previous chapters in this book, think about them, and make up your own list for consideration.

It is true that you will probably wish to spend some time in the social life of your church. I would suggest, however, that this not be the first priority. Even if you know several people in a particular congregation, that may not be the best reason for joining their church. You may be a serious inquirer, for example, whereas they may not be. It is a good rule to pick your social clubs for the people in them and for the activities they include; but pick your church because it is a good place for you to worship, to feel comfortable in worshipping, and to pursue your quest for Chris tian meaning for life.

I wish you all the best. One of the best proofs I know about for the truth of Christianity is that it works. It really does. In the next chapter, I propose to tell you a few general and specific instances in which I have seen Christianity work.

CHAPTER SEVEN
CHRISTIANITY WORKS

In Keith Miller's The Taste of New Wine, a group of people in a modern business decided to apply the words they believe in to their daily lives, including their actions as employees of that business. They find that it is possible to be Christians on the job as well as off. Gone is the kind of selfish motivation that previously they have believed to be necessary in business. Instead, now they treat customers and suppliers and colleagues fairly and honestly, putting the needs of others on a level no lower than their own needs.

They did not make such a large profit as they have before, Miller tells us, but they felt better about themselves and about being in business. Sometimes we think of life as requiring us to cut the throats of others around us; we call it 'the rat race' or worse and say that 'it's a jungle out there.' But it need not be.

Christianity works. That has been demonstrated over and over. But to live it requires genuine faith. It is easy to assume that it won't work, that it is too idealistic, and to adapt ourselves to the world around us. I have seen it work in large groups, in individual human beings, and in my own actions, sometimes when I have struggled against doing things the impractical way of Christianity. — I know that one cannot always trust other people; and I know that they do not always choose to trust me. But often I am surprised by the Christian actions of someone else. I am surprised, and my faith in Christianity and in other people is restored. I know that Christianity is practical, that it truly works, and that it can give meaning to one's live.

The Rotary Four-Way Test

There are many codes and sets of rules and slogans and moral platitudes in the atmosphere on American society. Many of them, I know, are ignored by the people who give lip service to them; perhaps most of them are just decorative ideas, meaningless fragments in our atmosphere. But one set of high moral principles has worked and, for many, keeps on working today. It is the Four-Way Test that every member of Rotary International promises faithfully to adopt as guiding principles in thoughts and actions.

Now, this does not mean that every member of Rotary understands and practices these four guidelines. I know better, of course. But they are something more than decorative slogans. Before they became official policy for all Rotary clubs in the world, they were used in business, so used as to pull that business out of bankruptcy.

At the bottom of the Depression, a man named Herbert Taylor took over a business that was ready to join the hundreds of other businesses in America that had gone under because of their financial plights. When Taylor took over that business, the had to put up most of his capital to obtain additional support from the banks and keep it alive. The company made aluminum pots and pans. So did a great many other companies. Taylor asked himself what could be done to make his company different from all those other companies around him. His company's products were no better — and no worse — than those made by other companies. So how could his company develop the trust of customers and stay alive? His answer was what has become the famous Four-Way Test:

1. Is it the truth?

2. Is it fair to all concerned?

3. Will it build good will and better friendships?

4. Will it be beneficial to all concerned?

Just as now all Rotarians are asked to make these four questions the guides of everything they think, say and do, Taylor asked all of the people in his business to make it their test. The result was trust. In this day when we sometimes wonder if we can trust anyone in a business or professional transaction, we would probably be willing to pay a good deal just to know that there was one organization we could deal with that we trust. If that organization (or individual professional) were to follow the standards above, we could! How wonderful! How valuable is the ability to trust!

Having been a member of four Rotary clubs, I know that not all Rotarians follow this rule. But I have known many who do, who take it seriously, just as I have known many Christians who take seriously the standards of the New Testament — not who invariably live up to them (even Paul could not quite do that, he tells us) — members of Christian churches who take the time and trouble to discover what the New Testament standards are and try to put them in practice in their own lives.

Christianity works.

Where did Taylor get these standards that turned his business around and made it financially solvent? — Well, it was never spelled out to most Rotarians until his death, in the 1970's, I believe. Then a news item reported that Taylor's death mentioned the fact that he had had a strong connection with a Christian church of some denomination, a connection he took seriously, one that had very much affected his life.

Christianity works!

When Taylor became the international president of Rotary, in the 1950's, he gave his four-way test to Rotary International. It had worked in his business; it could work for others, too.

Other Christian Practices in Business

Recently our Rotary club heard a Wal-Mart assistant manager talk about the ten principles that this large and very successful company has developed. I quote a few of them below:

5. We maintain a strong work ethic.

6. Our leaders are also servants.

7. We have integrity in all we do.

These principles suggest New Testament principles to me. But so do those principles governing attitudes toward and between customers and Wal-Mart employees and associates (employees) and coaches (supervisors). All human beings involved in the process are supposed to be treated with respect and consideration. All opinions are valued and may affect store practices and policies. This huge system of retail stores is not just a machine, each employee being a sort of cog in the machine.

Christianity works.

In the early 1980's, a book appeared on the best-seller lists by Thomas J. Peters and Robert H. Waterman, Jr., **Excellence**. It was an analysis of what the authors call 'lessons from America's best-run companies.' As I read through it, I was not amazed, for I had already seen some of these principles applied in the most successful school I had ever observed. But I am sure that those who believe that business must be a 'jungle,' one full of people eager to cut throats, may have been amazed. These best-run companies in America, in almost every case, treated workers and other human being with respect. The lowest employee ('lowest' in

117

salary or wages) could make a suggestion, and that suggestion would be considered; this policy is the kind that may seem astounding to those who have worked only for what I call 'fly-by-night' businesses, one step up from the criminal world. — And I mention such borderline businesses only because in past years high school students have often found their summer jobs with them and developed negative attitudes toward business in general as a result; I know this because the college students in English I once counseled on the job market often reported negative attitudes toward business in general. — Companies that really succeed, according to the editors of **Excellence**, often have policies and practices that we could trace back to the New Testament.

Christianity works.

Now, all through this book I have reminded you that Christians are not perfect and that you will never find a perfect church. But I do believe that churches in a community can and do make a difference. If you have ever viewed that Jimmy Stewart film, **It's A Wonderful Life**, you can guess what I mean. If you were to remove all churches and all church influence in any community for a generation or two, you would know what I mean. Some pessimists would even say that we can see signs of this decay now, but I believe that, as Dr. D. Elton Trueblood has said, 'We may be early Christians.' Time must have a different meaning for God and for human beings; what seems such a long time to us, almost two thou sand years since Jesus walked among us, may be insignificant in the mind of God.

And we do know that, over and over, the Jews first and the Christians later, went through lows as well as ap parent peaks of belief. The times we live in now may simply be a temporary low before a great leap forward. We cannot tell. But we need not be pessimistic.

Now I would like to tell you about a school I once observed closely, one in which Christians of various background worked together toward a great goal and definitely proved to me that Christianity works.

Washington Irving Junior High

From 1950 through 1957, I taught at Washington Irving Junior High in Des Moines, Iowa. We all worked very hard there; I can still remember the details of my own impossible schedule: first, a home room of 30 or so, then six 55-minute classes of an average of 36 1/2, English classes most years, for that was my major field. Because I taught the ninth grade advanced semester class (those who were to com plete junior high that semester), I also was assigned sponsorship of the school newspaper. It was published once a month during the school year and had a big edition at the end of the year with a photo of the graduates, notes on them, and statements by them. We had no typing classes, and our kids could not drive cars, so I typed all final copy and took it to the printer. I also met with editors and reporters and once each week met with home room representatives we called home room reporters. I was in the army reserve as a part time job, but I also had to be on a men's bowling team that bowled earlier in the evening on the reserve meeting night. (After the first two years, we added other men to the faculty, and I no longer had to bowl in order to make sure our school was represented by two teams.) Because I taught what we called the 9A's, I had to work with others on preparing the closing ceremonies for the school year; I was also on a certain number of assembly committees, sang in a men's quartet for P.T.A. meetings and some assemblies, and represented my school on certain district committees. In some of my years at Irving, I also had to supervise kids playing basketball in one of the two school gymnasiums from eight until noon on Saturdays. I say 'had to', for the regular week tired me out, and I would have been happy to sleep in on Saturdays; but if I did, a friend of mine would be left to supervise two gymnasiums by himself; we were paid the minimum wage for this by the city recreation board, so desperate as I often was for money, I could have stayed at home gladly.

That was my schedule. It was the best school I ever taught in, and I have taught in some good schools.

For one thing, whatever egos we had were kept subdued because our work was directed not at personal aggrandizement, but at getting the job done, fulfilling the worthy goals we had as a school. Irving was what is now called an inner city school. Four out of five students came from homes at the poverty level. Irving had the highest percentage of minority students in the city, at least at the secondary level. We all very much wanted our students to achieve the best that could be achieved. We believed in them and in what we were doing. I suppose we simply did not have time to be very much concerned about ourselves and our own egos. Yet the quality of the faculty members was very high.

All of us must have been concerned about money at some time before accepting jobs in Des Moines, for the city was the largest in the state and paid one of the top salaries. But on the job we were free to cooperate with other people around us, for we had a salary schedule that depended on degrees, college credits, and length of service in the system. Because no one had to waste time in polishing the apple for a bonus, and no one felt it necessary to keep secret whatever good ideas worked in practice, we did a great deal of sharing, but most of all, we were motivated by trying to do the impossible. We gave it our best.

Only incidentally did I learn of the religious backgrounds of the people on the faculty. (Naturally, we did not want to know about the churches our pupils attended or whether they attended church or not. We made it a matter of pride not to be influenced in any way by race, sex, creed, or political connections; so I simply do not know what my pupils or their parents did about worship or voting.) The woman teacher who handled the fund drives to support our newspaper, and who taught business at Irving, was Miss Laverne Cullen; she was a conscientious Catholic. Three of our faculty members were active in United Methodist Churches. On our faculty were Presbyterians, Disciples of Christ, Baptists, Lutherans, Independent Christians, and members of other denominations that I cannot remember or never knew; I simply knew that they were Christian in their beliefs and that they put their faith into practice on the job.

Perhaps a thumb-nail description of a few of them would be of some use; Dr. Warren Nixon was our principal for most of my time at Irving and for some years after I left. Some people would call him naive, innocent, unsophisticated; I'm sure of that. Such people identify being street wise with being wise. As a former boys' vice principal at Irving, Dr. Nixon was hardly innocent of the corruption and evil in the world; he was, however, innocent in his simple faith that if you tried to do the right thing, most of the time it would work out well. At Irving it did; certainly it did when he was principal. Dr. Nixon had graduated from a Des Moines high school at fifteen because he was very bright. He had attended Irving before that end, in spite of his youth, had been on a record-breaking relays team. At Drake University, he had majored in economics, which later he taught in a Des Moines high school; but he had so excelled in track and field events (at the famous Drake Relays, for example) that he had a lifetime pass to all Drake University athletic events, awarded to him for his record as an athlete at Drake. He taught me — and I think the rest of the faculty as well — a great deal about being a Christian. For example, in our weekly faculty meetings on Wednesday mornings, he left it entirely up to us as to what we would do as a school, the only stipulation being that we stay within the very broad and general rules established by the Des Moines Board of Education. He did not impose his ideas on us, but left us to consider only the good of the students and how we could best help them. We were loyal to him and to one another; we worked harder than we ever would have done if we had been working for selfish purposes or to please some selfish principal. — I should point out that Dr. Nixon did not start the democratic system then in practice in Des Moines schools, but he knew it well and took it to the limits. It worked. Because we all trusted him and trusted one another, I know it was truly Christian. No one had to tell me that.

Another great Christian on the faculty was Miss Marjorie Waite. Like Dr. Nixon and my old friends Mr. Oldham and Mr. Pennington, she was a member of the United Methodist denomination. I know that sometimes she was disapproving of me and of others like me, for she was a sort of Methodist nun — that a nun of the 1950's. Yet she understood us, in a sense, and she recognized our hard work and our potential for growth. At Irving we had one of the area's secondary school EMR groups (the educable mentally retarded.) As I recall, all of them had IQ's below 80; I do not know what the lowest scores were. Miss Waite and Miss Lambert and Mr. Hoffmand and some other teachers worked with them, Miss Bird, for one. All of them were great people, but I think all of them would agree that Miss Waite was the most dedicated. Anecdotes come to mind to illustrate her dedication, but I will not take up space to relate them here. I simply know how dedicated she was. While I was still on the faculty, but not long before she retired, she treated herself to one long trip, by air and rail. It was typical of her and of her life: She took a trip around the world to visit Untied Methodist missions in other countries. — Not my idea of a pleasure tour, but then I am not so Godly as Miss Waite was. But without being so Godly, I could nevertheless admire her, as others did.

She retired after I moved to California to teach, but a mutual friend on the faculty told me what she did on retiring: She bought a small house in the slums of Des Moines and worked very hard to keep it clean and the house painted and the yard neat and well trimmed. She did it at minimum cost and in order to set an example for the poor people around her. She forced herself to live on precisely the amount given to the poor who were on welfare, using her other funds for good purposes. Whenever she found that the amount allowed by the state government was too small for people to live on, she organized and led a peaceful but firm protest on the state capitol, also in Des Moines. I do not know her politics, but I am almost sure that she was a republican. She took both her religion and her politics seriously and tried to make them work in practice.

I could give even more details about Miss Edna McCutcheon, a good friend and colleague on the faculty. In her own way, she was my teacher, one of the best I ever had. But she was a Presbyterian and a member of my own church, so I should not tell so much about her inasmuch as it might be considered a plug for my own denomination, which it most certainly would not be intended to be. But Miss McCutcheon, in my book, was a saint.

If I were to go on listing people here, I would be sure to omit some who were wonderful Christians. I do not wish to do so. So I will leave those names with you as representatives of the faculty, better than the rest of us, probably, but still representative.

Much of what I learned about Christianity was in observing the actions of faculty members at Washington Irving Junior High.

Christianity works.

But of course, we have to believe. We have to have faith that it will work, no matter what the wisdom of the street says, and we have to give it a try.

I could name as great Christians members of my family, members of the church in which I grew up, and members of every church I have been associated with since that time.

Christianity works. But it does take faith.

As I wrote all of this, I thought of some pastors I have known who have been saints, like Miss McCutcheon and others I have named. But if I have not named them, or seemed to remember them, I need not worry; for God, I'm sure knows them well.

Because teaching at Irving Junior High was so demanding of me, I eventually left, eventually obtained a doctorate, and eventually spent more than twenty years as a teacher at college and university levels. But I have never taught in a better school than Irving, either before or since, and I have never worked in and with a better group of people. They were dedicated Christians. There are many paradoxes in the New Testament, one of which was illustrated at Irving Junior High. I have mentioned it elsewhere; it appears in the words of Jesus in **Matthew 11:28-30**. We can all accept the first part of the statement readily enough; each of us feel depressed at times by the burdens of this world, and we seek help; Jesus offers that help, that rest. What seems illogical to us, with our human ways of thinking, our strictly human ways of thinking, our strictly human (and imperfect) logic, is what follows; for Jesus tells us right away to take His yoke upon us — another burden! — And just after we have been told that He offers us rest.

At Irving Junior High, we learned the meaning of that passage. Never have I worked so hard in my life as I did at Irving. And during those years, we had every burden we could imagine having; yet we got through. I think it was because we had little time to think of ourselves, much time to think of others.

I learned something about being a teacher at Irving, even more about being a Christian.

CHAPTER EIGHT
SHORT READING LIST

You will want to visit churches, quite a variety of them, I hope. But church visits are not nearly enough to help you make up your mind about where you can best pursue your serious study of Christian meaning for your life. You will need books as well. The following types I believe are very important for you to have and to study as you make up your mind:

A good translation of the Bible.

A good concordance to fit that Bible.

A good dictionary for the Bible.

A good commentary on the Bible to fit your denomination.

A book or pamphlet that tells the special nature of the denomination.

If you have pretty well decided which church you plan to join, you should see the pastor (or a pastor at another church of the same denomination) and get recommendations for each of the above. If you have not yet gone that far toward a particular church, you may want to borrow from a library or even purchase for your own use books from one of the following lists.

As to a concordance, I know only one, **Cruden's Concordance**, although I also have a much shorter one based on the Revised Standard translation of the Bible, but there are so many translations around now that I think a copy of Cruden's — used with your Bible plus the King James version — should be enough. If your priest or pastor recommends another one, then that is the one you should use.

If you have not narrowed your search to a particular denomination yet, then you may wish to try the following books in your study:

For Roman Catholics

The New American Bible, St. Joseph Edition.

The Jerome Biblical Commentary.

The Catholic Catechism, by John A Harden, S.J. (My paperback is 623 pages.)

Catholic Christianity, by Richard Chilson (newer)

If I were a Catholic, I would buy all of the books listed above. In fact, I do own them all now.

For Mainline Protestants

The Revised Standard translation of the Bible.

Either Harper's or the Westminster Dictionary of the Bible.

Harper's Commentary.

We own all of the above and use them regularly.

Like most mainline Protestant pastors, I also refer to the twelve-volume **Interpreter's Bible.** Many like **The Interpreter's Dictionary of the Bible**, in several volumes, but I rely mainly on Westminster.

For Conservative Protestants

The Good News translation of the Bible seems to be very popular.

Halley's Handbook is an old standby. Even older, but beautifully written, is Matthew Henry's Commentary. Pastors who are my friends have recommended Tyndale's and Eerdman's Bible dictionaries and Broadman's and Eerdman's commentaries.

In General

There are many, many Bible translations and quite a few dictionaries of the Bible and commentaries on it; beyond those listed above, however, I would suggest that you follow the recommendations of a pastor or priest you feel you can depend on.

Catholics place somewhat less emphasis on scripture than most Protestants do, but the books above should be useful. For specific information about a particular denomination, go to the pastor of a church of that denomination. I have short histories of such denominations as Presbyterians, Methodist, Church of God, Mennonites, Episcopalians, and one branch of the Baptists; but as you can see, those few denominations just scratch the surface of the denominations in America.

It is important, however, to understand the power structure of the denomination you choose as well as something of its history. Both of these can be factors in helping you decide whether or not to join.

Some New Testament Books

To find out what Christianity is and how it can guide you in your own life, it is a good idea to read carefully certain books of the New Testament using the appropriate references listed above. The entire New Testament will not take you long to read. To study it carefully is another matter, of course. I would recommend as a minimum reading list the following:

The Gospel of Matthew. (Basic.)

The Gospel of John. (Sometimes called a theological approach.)

Paul's Letter to the Romans (Paul's theology, some say.)

Reading for Enjoyment

Some of these books were startling when they first appeared, but most are now pretty well accepted by most Christians as good inspirational reading. I have liked them, and you may, too:

C. S. Lewis, **Mere Christianity** and **Surprised by Joy** and **Reflections on the Psalms**, and (quite different) **The Screwtape Letters**.

D. Elton Trueblood, **The Company and the Committed** and **Alternative to Futility**.

Leslie Weatherhead, **The Will of God** (one attempt to explain pain and suffering in God's world.)

Keith Miller, **The Taste of New Wine.**

J. B. Phillips, **Your God is Too Small.**

Karl Menninger, **What Ever Became of Sin?**

Paul Tournier, **Escape from Loneliness.**

As one who reads much, I should like you to remember that reading about Christian living is not the same as living as a Christian. It is, I think, a helpful preface, but not the real thing.

Good reading!

APPENDIX A:
CHURCHES WE VISITED

Between July of 1991 and July of 1993, Mrs. Otto and I visited one hundred churches. We had originally planned to stop at the end of fifty visits, but some of our friends did not seem to feel that fifty visits would tell us much. Consequently, we visited another fifty. We learned something, we felt, from every visit, so doubling the original total of fifty was probably a good idea. Since we concluded our program of visits, we have been able to detect (silently, of course) mistaken stereotypes in the opinions of intelligent, educated people, as well as in certain television presentations and newspaper and magazine references. Naturally, visits cannot be a substitute for reading; but I do feel that they are an often neglected form of research, a form that gives a certain balance to the whole.

These are the churches we visited:

Roman Catholic

Holy Cross Catholic, Champaign, Illinois
St. James Catholic, Decatur, Illinois
St. Mary's Catholic, Champaign, Illinois
Lourdes Catholic, Decatur, Illinois
Immaculate Conception Catholic, St. Mary's, Indiana
St. Anthony's Catholic, Effingham, Illinois
Forty Martyrs Catholic, Tuscola, Illinois
St. Mary's Catholic, Paris, Illinois
St. John's Catholic, Arcola, Illinois

Episcopal

Emmanuel Episcopal, Champaign, Illinois
Galilee Episcopal, Virginia Beach, Virginia
Trinity Episcopal, Mattoon, Illinois
Cathedral of St. Paul, Springfield, Illinois

United Methodist Churches

First Methodist, Urbana, Illinois
First United Methodist, Oakland, Illinois
First United Methodist, Champaign, Illinois
Maple Avenue United Methodist, Terre Haute, Indiana
Union United Methodist, Quincy, Illinois
Ocran United Methodist, Sutherland, Virginia
Grace United Methodist, Decatur, Illinois

Free Methodist

Bradbury Free Methodist, Toledo, Illinois
Moundford Free Methodist, Decatur, Illinois
Free Methodist, Mattoon, Illinois
Free Methodist, Bethany, Illinois

Nazarene

First Nazarene, Mattoon, Illinois
First Church of Nazarene, Decatur, Illinois

Lutheran (Evangelical)

Mount Olivet Lutheran, Minneapolis, Minnesota
Trinity Evangelical Lutheran, Monticello, Minnesota
Luther Memorial, Quincy, Illinois
St. Matthew's Lutheran, Urbana, Illinois

Lutheran (Missouri Synod)

St. Paul's Lutheran, Decatur, Illinois
St. John's Lutheran, Champaign, Illinois
Grace Lutheran, Paris, Illinois
Trinity Lutheran, Urbana, Illinois

United Church of Christ

United Church of Christ, St. Charles, Missouri
United Church of Christ, Tuscola, Illinois
Bethany United Church of Christ, West Terra Haute, Indiana
St. Peter's United Church of Christ, Champaign, Illinois
Congregational Church (U.C.C.), Faribault, Minnesota

Disciples of Christ

First Christian Church, Mattoon, Illinois
Vine Street Christian Church, Arthur, Illinois
First Christian Church, Minneapolis, Minnesota
First Christian Church, Bethany, Illinois

Independent Christian

South Side Christian Church, Springfield, Illinois
Mattoon Christian Church, Mattoon, Illinois
Broadway Christian Church, Mattoon, Illinois
First Christian Church, Kansas, Illinois
First Christian Church, Windsor, Illinois
Eastview Christian Church, Bloomington, Illinois

Church of Christ

Highway Church of Christ, Sullivan, Illinois
Lake Land Church of Christ, Mattoon, Illinois

American Baptist

First Baptist Church, Urbana, Illinois
First Baptist Church, Savoy, Illinois
First Baptist Church, Mattoon, Illinois

Southern Baptist

First Baptist Church, Westfield, Illinois
First Baptist Church, Mt. Zion, Illinois
Elm Street Baptist Church, Petersburg, Virginia
First Southern Baptist, Mattoon, Illinois
Emmaus Baptist Church, Quinton, Virginia
First Baptist Church, Clarksville, Illinois

Mennonite

North Vine Street Mennonite Church, Arthur, llinois
Sunnyside Church (rural), Arthur, Illinois

Church of God

Mound Chapel Church of God, Decatur, Illinois
First Church of God, Sullivan, Illinois

129

Christian Missionary and Alliance

Champaign Alliance Church, Champaign, Illinois
First Alliance Church, Mattoon, Illinois

Holiness

Wesley Church, Charleston, Illinois

Pentecostal

Fourth Street Pentecostal, Effingham, Illinois

Assembly of God

First Assembly of God, Mattoon, Illinois
Calvary Assembly of God, Decatur, Illinois
First Assembly of God, Terre Haute, Illinois
Campus Crossroads Church, Champaign, Illinois
First Assembly of God, Effingham, Illinois
Calvary Temple, Springfield, Illinois

Unitarian-Universalist

Unitarian Church, Quincy, Illinois
Unitarian Church, Decatur, Illinois
Unitarian-Universalist Church, Urbana, Illinois

Community Churches

Virginia Beach Community Chapel, Virginia Beach, Virginia
Central Community Church, Mattoon, Illinois

Salvation Army

Salvation Army, Decatur, Illinois
Salvation Army, Champaign, Illinois

Presbyterian Church

Westminster Presbyterian, Decatur, Illinois
First Presbyterian, Greenville, Illinois
First Presbyterian, Virginia Beach, Virginia
First Presbyterian Church, Springfield, Illinois

First Presbyterian Church, Effingham, Illinois
First Presbyterian Church, Champaign, Illinois
First Presbyterian Church, St. Cloud, Minnesota
First Presbyterian Church, Mt. Zion, Illinois

Christian Reformed

Hassel Park Christian Reformed Church, Champaign, Illinois

Greek Orthodox

Hellenic Greek Orthodox, Decatur, Illinois

Full Gospel

Calvary Full Gospel, Seelyville, Indiana

Independent Bible

Stratford Park Bible Church, Champaign, Illinois

Christian Science

First Christian Science Church, Champaign, Illinois
First Christian Science Church, Terre Haute, Illinois

Evangelical Free Church

Evangelical Free Church, Decatur, Illinois

Unity Church

Urbana Unity Church, Urbana, Illinois

Latter Day Saints

Latter Day Saints Church, Mattoon, Illinois

Friends (Quaker)

Friends Meeting House, Urbana, Illinois

Reformed

Crystal Cathedral, Garden Grove, California

While we were visiting these churches on Sundays, I made appointments with twenty pastors, mainly pastors of these churches, and interviewed them at length (for about two hours each), using a questionnaire that I had prepared in advance and had, in most cases, mailed to them in advance. Just as we had tried to visit churches that in general represented the churches Americans attend, I tried to interview pastors who were representative of those churches. All of the pastors interviewed were good at their work, but many good pastors were not interviewed, generally because I wished the persons interviewed to be representative.

The list of pastors interviewed is on the next page.

Pastors Interviewed

Rev. Bob Clark, First Christian Church (Disciples), Mattoon, Illinois
Rev. Terry Davis, First Baptist Church (Southern), Mt. Zion, Illinois
Rev. Lynn Denison, Maple Avenue United Methodist Church, Terre Haute, Illinois
Rev. Mike Goar, Charleston Community Church, Charleston, Illinois
Rev. Jacob Graber, Sunnyside Mennonite Church, Arthur, Illinois
Rev. Scottie Griffin, First Presbyterian Church, Virginia Beach, Virginia
Rev. Al Groner, First Southern Baptist Church, Mattoon, Illinois
Rev. John Grossoehme, First Alliance Church, Mattoon, Illinois
Rev. Martin Gutzmer, Oakland-Hindsboro United Methodist, Oakland, Illinois
Rev. Drew Holloway, First Presbyterian Church, Effingham, Illinois
Rev. Michael Johnson, Vine Street Christian Church, Arthur, Illinois (Disc.)
Rev. Joe Latson, Bradbury Free Methodist Church, Toledo, Illinois
Rev. Don Lemkau, (Retired) United Methodist Church, Charleston, Illinois
Rev. Gordon McLean, First Presbyterian Church, Springfield, Illinois
Rev. C. Q. McMillion, Mound Chapel Church of God, Decatur, Illinois
Rev. (Father) Joe Ring, Forty Martyrs Catholic Church, Tuscola, Illinois
Rev. (Father) Thomas Royer, St. Mary's Catholic Church, Champaign, Illinois
Rev. Lee Stauff, Stratford Park Bible Chapel, Champaign, Illinois
Rev. Lynn Smith-Roberts, Macomb and Quincy Unitarian-Universalist, Macomb, Illinois
Rev. Don Wallace, First Assembly of God Church, Effingham, Illinois

APPENDIX B:
SOME DANGERS OF THEOLOGY

An atheist friend of mine once remarked, 'All of the wars in history have been started because of religion.' My first reaction was that of a smart alec; I said, 'If you count your discipline (economics) as a religion — and many economists treat it that way — you may be right.' Even with that qualification, however, I was probably wrong. For some wars, I am sure, have not been started over either the religiously held views of competitors on economic problems or over differing interpretations of the mind of God. Yet I believe he was partly correct.

Over the centuries, we have often burned heretics at the stake, people who held different views from ours about the nature and the mind of God. I would not blame those burnings or the many religious wars we have had on God or on religion, however; for theology is the systematic working out by one or more human — hence, imperfect — minds of God's perfect mind. Writing in a book, Man's Unconquerable Mind, which is really not about religion, the distinguished scholar and classicist Gilbert Highet says, 'Every human mind is drastically limited.' (p. 104) Elsewhere in the same book he says that all philosophers of importance have agreed that human beings are im perfect. If we accept his conclusions about the human mind, then we must also conclude that it was the fatuous pride of human beings in their theologies that caused them to murder others in religious persecutions and wars; it was not God. I would suggest, then, that there is danger in placing too much confidence in whatever theology we accept. We may be wrong. History tells us that we often have been wrong; we may be sure that we shall be wrong in the present and the future.

Now, I say all of this in part because the seminaries I have visited seem to have placed greater emphasis on theology in the last fifty years, in part because in my own denomination and in some others I know a good deal about, I see delegates running off to assemblies and parliaments of one sort or another all too eager to pass dozens of resolutions without much study in advance, resolutions based on com mittee reports and recommendations, without really knowing that they are saying in those resolutions that 'This is what God thinks.' Sometimes such resolutions result in their own kinds of wars, wars that can even cost lives and that can certainly steal time away from prayer and the daily practice of Christianity.

In the meantime, tolerance for the opinions of our neighbors is not much in fashion.

Yet knowing that theology is made up of the conclusions of imperfect minds, we should be tolerant. Tolerant and humble.

One of the best-known theologians of the twentieth century, Karl Barth, cautions all theologians to be humble about whatever opinions they may derive from their study, for he says that all theology is human and that all human theology is imperfect. (Evangelical Theology: Introduction p.113 et al). He is right to do so. I could list hundreds of sad instances of misguided actions taken by rash human beings in the name of theology, but I should think that individual reflection should call up enough examples to any educated mind so that I would not have to do so.

Every denomination has some sort of theological conclusions as the basis for religion. Probably such a basis is necessary; otherwise, we might be left with a quarter of a billion individual theologies in the United States alone. But we do need to be tolerant and humble.

In my own denomination, Presbyterian, I have often heard pastors say that they would have difficulty in accepting our creeds and catechisms without a good deal of strain in their definition of terms. If those who are paid to be Christians feel this way, it is all the more reason why those of us who are simply church members should have somewhat erratic opinions tolerated, so long as we have a degree of humility about those opinions.

Some theologians, Hans Kung, for example, believe that we should at least use scripture as the base for our theological opinions. But even then, as history must teach us, we have difficulties in reaching agreement. Early in the nineteenth century, an American preacher named Alexander Campbell felt that all Christians could be brought together in one church if we would only follow this simple rule: 'Where the scriptures speak, we speak; where the scriptures are silent, we are silent.' It was a noble effort, but as one of Campbell's modern followers has pointed out, the Campbellites did not bring in other religious groups. Instead, they split, repeatedly. If anything should teach us humility, that example alone should.

It is important for each of us to work out his or her own theology, but then to be tentative and humble about the result.